BUSINESS LEADERSHIP STYLES

Discover Personality Traits and Increase Success, Retention and Profits

Diane Schildgen, PhD

Copyright © 2024 by Diane Schildgen. All rights reserved.

No part of this publication may be reproduced, distributed, or transmitted in any form or by any means, including photocopying, recording, or other electronic or mechanical methods, without the prior written permission of the author, except in the case of brief quotations embodied in critical reviews and certain other noncommercial uses permitted by copyright law.

Business Leadership Styles, Author: Diane Schildgen. — 1st ed.

Printed in the United States of America

First Printing, 2024

"Business Leadership Styles" is a transformative guide for leaders and managers seeking to unlock their team's full potential and drive organizational success.

A research-backed framework is presented that enables readers to identify and leverage the unique strengths of their team members, fostering a thriving culture of collaboration and innovation.

Filled with real-world examples and practical strategies, this book provides a roadmap for adapting leadership styles to meet the organization's needs, maximizing potential, boosting retention, and increasing profits.

The five most typical styles will be surveyed by the first portion of the *DCS5 Personality Assessments*.

Whether you're a seasoned executive or a first-time manager, "Business Leadership Styles" offers the tools to bring out the best in your people and take your organization to new heights.

It was time to do our science fair presentation, but my partner never showed up. We got an 'F'.

*When my 14-year-old self, asked,
"Why do I have to take the blame? It wasn't my fault."*

"Because you were in charge. It was your responsibility."

"But, that's not fair."

"Do you like being in charge?"

"Well, yeah."

"Sometimes, it's hard to be the leader."

To my father, Don Schildgen

Table of Contents

INTRODUCTION 1

CHAPTER 1
THE ESSENCE OF LEADERSHIP IN BUSINESS 3

1.1 Defining Leadership in the Modern Business Environment 4

Evolving Leadership Patterns: 4
Sustainability and Leadership: 4

1.2 The Psychological Impact of Leadership Styles on Employee Performance 5

Well-being: 5
Motivation: 5
Emotional intelligence: 5
Feedback Culture: 6

1.3 Balancing Empathy with Authority: A Key Leadership Skill 6

Empathy as Strength: 6
Boundaries: 7
Difficult Conversations: 7
Motivation's Science: 8

1.4 The Science of Motivation: Understanding What Drives Your Team 9

Decoding Motivation: 9
Personalization of Motivation: 10
The Role of Autonomy: 11
Recognition and Reward Systems: 11

CHAPTER 2
LEADERSHIP STYLES EXPLORED 13

2.1 Servant Leadership: Putting Your Team First 13
Principles: 13
Servant Leadership in Practice: 14
Challenges: 14
Measuring the Impact: 15

2.2 The Dynamics of Democratic Leadership in a Corporate Setting 15
Features: 15
Benefits: 16
Challenges and Limitations: 16
Case Studies: 17

2.3 Authoritarian Leadership: When is it Effective? 17
Definitions: 17
Appropriate Contexts: 18
Risks and Pitfalls: 18
Balancing authority with compassion: 19
Assessment: 19

2.4 Laissez-Faire Leadership: Autonomy and Trust at Play 20
Understanding Laissez-Faire Leaders: 20
Potential Drawbacks: 21
Ideal Conditions: 22
Accountability: 22
Respect and Trust: 23

2.5 Charismatic Leadership: The Power of Persuasion and Vision 24
Characteristics: 24
Influence on Morale: 25
Dangers: 25
Sustaining Success: 26

CHAPTER 3
ADAPTING LEADERSHIP TO TEAM DYNAMICS 28

3.1 Cultural Diversity in Teams: Leading with Sensitivity 29
Enhancing Cultural Differences: 29
Sensitivity Training: 29

Customized Communication: 30
Celebrating Diversity: 30
Challenges and Opportunities: 31

3.2 The Generational Mix: Bridging the Gap with Adaptive Leadership 32

Understanding Generations: 32
Adaptive Techniques: 33
Mentoring: 33
Technology: 34

3.3 Remote Leadership: Strategies for the Digital Age 35

Effective Communication: 35
Remote Management: 36
Building Virtual Teams: 37
Assessment: 37
Work-Life Balance: 39

3.4 Crisis Leadership: Steering Your Team Through Turmoil 39

Preparedness and Resilience: 40
Empathy: 41
Ready to Adapt: 41
Post-Crisis: 42

3.5 Feedback Loops: Encouraging Open Communication 42

Feedback Culture: 43
Techniques: 44
Act On It: 44
Continuous Improvement: 45

3.6 Working with Volunteers 46

Motivation: 46
Accountability: 47
Retention and Turnover: 47
Training and development: 48

CHAPTER 4
BUILDING AND SUSTAINING HIGH-PERFORMANCE TEAMS 49

4.1 Setting Clear Goals and Expectations in a Transparent Manner 50

The Importance of Clarity: 50

Transparency in Goal Setting: 51
Regular Progress Reviews: 51
Celebrating Achievements: 52

4.2 Recognizing and Utilizing the Strengths of Each Team Member 53

Strengths-Based Leadership: 54
Personalized Role Design: 55
Feedback: 56

4.3 The Art of Delegation: Empowerment without Abdication 56

Clear Communication: 57
Empowerment: 57
Avoid Micromanagement: 57

4.4 Conflict Resolution: Maintaining Harmony and Productivity . 58

Proactive and Mediate: 59
Building a Resilient Culture: 59

4.5 The Role of Continuous Learning in Team Development 60

Lifelong Learning: 61
Personalized Plans: 61
Learning From Success and Failure 62

CHAPTER 5
PERSONAL DEVELOPMENT FOR LEADERS 64

5.1 Self-Assessment Tools for Leadership Styles and Impact 64

Strengths and Areas of Growth: 64
Actionable Insights: 66

5.2 Embracing Vulnerability as a Strength 66

Authenticity: 66
Team Bonding: 67
Safe Space for Sharing: 68
Vulnerable Moments 69

5.3 Time Management: Leading by Example 70

Balance: 70
Prioritize: 71
Boundaries: 72

5.4 Nurturing Emotional Intelligence for Better Leadership 72

Emotional Intelligence (EI): 72
Empathy: 73
Conflict Resolution: 73

5.5 The Leader as a Coach: Developing Future Leaders 74

Coaching for Growth: 74
Mentoring vs. Coaching: 75
Feedback that Promotes Development: 75
Individual Development Plans: 76

CHAPTER 6
FOSTERING A CULTURE OF INNOVATION AND GROWTH 78

6.1 Encouraging Risk-Taking and Learning from Failure 79

Fostering a Safe Environment for Experimentation: 80
The Role of Failure in Innovation: 81
Celebrating Attempts, Not Just Successes: 81
Learning and Adapting from Missteps: 82

6.2 The Importance of Vision Casting in Inspiring Innovation 82

Creating and Communicating a Compelling Vision: 83
Aligning Team Efforts with Vision: 84
Storytelling in Vision Casting: 85
Revisiting and Revising the Vision: 85

6.3 Leveraging Diversity for Creative Problem Solving 86

Value of Diverse Perspectives: 87
Inclusivity: 87
Unconscious Bias: 88
Diverse Teams: 89

6.4 Creating Spaces for Collaboration and Co-creation 89

Sessions: 90
Building a Culture of Co-creation: 90

CHAPTER 7
ETHICS, INTEGRITY, AND TRANSPARENCY 92

7.1 Ethical Decision Making: A Guide for Leaders 93

Frameworks for Ethical Decision Making: 94
Balancing Stakeholder Interests: 95

Ethical Dilemmas in Leadership: 95
The Role of Values in Ethical Leadership: 96
Ethical Decision-Making Exercise: 96

7.2 Building and Maintaining Trust through Transparency 97

A Foundation for Trust: 98
Practical Transparency Practices: 99
The Impact of Transparency on Trust: 100
Rebuilding Trust through Transparency: 101

7.3 Integrity in Leadership: Actions Speak Louder than Words .. 101

Consistency Between Words and Actions: 102
Consequences of Compromising: 103
Integrity Under Pressure: 104
Modeling Integrity: 104

7.4 The Impact of Ethical Leadership on Company Culture 105

Shaping the Culture: 105
An Ethical Environment: 106
Ethical Leadership and Employee Satisfaction: 106

7.5 Leading by Example: Ethical Practices in Daily Operations .. 108

Daily Decisions: 108
Crisis Situations: 109
Training and Development: 110
Monitoring and Enforcing Ethical Standards: 111

CHAPTER 8
COMMUNICATING EFFECTIVELY AS A LEADER 113

8.1 Active Listening Skills for Effective Leadership 114

Fundamentals of Active Listening: 115
Improving Emotional Intelligence Through Listening: 115
Active Listening Techniques: 116
Overcoming Barriers: 116

8.2 Adapting Communication Styles to Your Audience 117

Adapting Your Communication Style 118
Tailoring Messages: 119
Across Generations: 120

8.3 Navigating Difficult Conversations with Grace and Authority 121

Preparation: 122
Maintaining Composure and Authority: 123
Constructive Outcomes: 123
Following Up After Difficult Conversations 124

8.4 Utilizing Technology for Clear and Consistent Communication
.... 124

Digital: 125
Digital Challenges: 125
Best Practices: 125

CHAPTER 9
LEADERSHIP IN STRATEGIC PLANNING AND EXECUTION 127

9.1 Aligning Team Efforts with Organizational Goals 127

Clarifying Organizational Vision and Goals: 128
Strategies for Effective Alignment: 129
Successful Alignment: 130

9.2 Strategic Decision-Making: Balancing Short-term Needs with Long-Term Vision 131

Strategic Decision Making: 132
The Role of Data in Strategic Decisions: 133
Navigating Trade-offs and Compromises: 133
Developing a Strategic Mindset: 134

9.3 Leading Change: Strategies for Effective Implementation 135

Change Principles: 136
Resistance To Change: 137
Role of Leaders: 138
Evaluation: 138

9.4 Measuring Success: KPIs for Leadership and Team Performance 139

Identifying Relevant KPIs: 140
Set Clear Targets: 141
Continuous Improvement: 142
Balancing Quantitative and Qualitative Measures 142

9.5 Succession Planning: Preparing for Leadership Transitions .. 143

Importance of a Plan: 143
Steps in Developing a Succession Plan: 144

Succession Challenges: 145
Advantages: 146

CHAPTER 10
CULTIVATING LEADERSHIP AT EVERY LEVEL 147

10.1 Identifying and Nurturing Potential Leaders Within Your Team 148

Spotting Leadership Potential: 149
Tailored Development Opportunities: 150
Empowering Emerging Leaders: 151

10.2 Creating a Leadership Development Program: Key Components and Best Practices 152

Designing Leadership Programs: 153
Integrating with Strategy: 153
Measuring the Success: 154
Continuously Improving: 155

10.3 Leadership and Legacy: Leaving a Mark on Your Organization 156

The Legacy: 156
Building a Lasting Legacy 156
Organizational Culture: 157
Case Studies: 157

CHAPTER 11
21 ADDITIONAL STYLES 160

Agile Leadership: 161
Bureaucratic Leadership: 163
Change Leadership: 164
Collaborative Leadership: 166
Customer-centric Leadership: 168
Entrepreneurial Leadership: 170
Environmental Leadership: 172
Holacratic Leadership: 173
Innovative Leadership: 175
Knowledge Leadership: 177
Lean Leadership: 179
Performance Leadership: 180
Risk Leadership: 182
Situational Leadership: 184
Supply Chain Leadership: 185

Strategic Leadership: 187
Team-based Leadership: 189
Transactional Leadership: 190
Transformational Leadership: 192
Quality Leadership: 194
Virtual Leadership: 195

CHAPTER 12
DETERMINE YOUR STYLE (AVOID PITFALLS) DCS5 PERSONALITY ASSESSMENTS 197

12.1 What To Avoid 197

12.2 DCS5 Personality Assessment: Time to Take the Survey 200

12.3 Servant Leadership 202

12.4 Democratic Leadership 211

12.5 Authoritarian Leadership 220

12.6 Laissez-Faire Leadership 229

12.7 Charismatic Leadership 238

DCS5 Personality Assessment Results 247

CONCLUSION 248

REFERENCES 252

"Leadership can appear anywhere in an organization. Your leaders might be in the penthouse suite, at the manager level, or in entry-level positions. Leadership is more about influence rather than power."

-- Diane Schildgen

Introduction

Companies globally lose around $1 trillion annually due to employees voluntarily leaving their jobs. This highlights leadership's profound effect on an organization's profitability. This book aims to address this critical issue by offering practical insights and strategies to improve workplace dynamics.

The author has over five decades of leadership experience across various industries and volunteer organizations. They have witnessed firsthand how effective management can revitalize underperforming teams, boost morale, and drive financial success. This book explores five primary leadership styles (servant, laissez-faire, democratic, authoritarian, charismatic) and briefly introduces twenty-one additional styles. It provides a toolkit to enhance team cohesion, morale, and productivity with practical applications and five sections of the **DCS5 Personality Assessment.**

The book integrates personal examples, ethical considerations, real-world applications, and self-assessment tools. It emphasizes the importance of integrity-based leadership through personal experiences navigating ethical dilemmas. As you dig deeper into leadership exploration, be prepared to transform how you lead by engaging with the material and considering your own qualities. The journey to becoming an inspiring, effective leader is worthwhile.

"Leadership is the capacity to translate vision into reality. The manager asks how and when; the leader asks what and why."

- Warren Bennis, American scholar, organizational consultant, and author, widely regarded as a pioneer of the contemporary field of leadership studies.

Chapter 1
The Essence of Leadership in Business

A newly appointed CEO must reignite a once-innovative company's spirit and drive growth, illustrating leadership's critical modern business role. Effective leadership significantly impacts organizational success.

Empathy enhances a leader's authority by building trust and understanding team dynamics. The chapter explains balancing empathy with enforcing boundaries and navigating difficult conversations. It describes motivational science, personalization strategies, autonomy's role, and effective recognition/reward systems design.

The chapter explores nuanced leadership dynamics influencing organizational culture, employee well-being, motivation, and ultimate business success. Masterfully applied, these principals can inspire teams to innovate while nurturing an engaging, empathetic work environment.

1.1 Defining Leadership in the Modern Business Environment

Evolving Leadership Patterns:

The digital era, characterized by rapid technological advances and global interconnectivity, has ushered in new leadership challenges and opportunities. Today's landscape demands adaptability, as change is the only constant. Critical traits for modern leaders include digital literacy, cross-cultural competence, and the ability to champion digital transformations, leverage data analytics, and manage globally dispersed teams. These evolving paradigms require leaders to be continual learners and innovators who don't just respond to changes but anticipate and lead transitions themselves.

Sustainability and Leadership:

The modern business landscape is increasingly prioritizing sustainability and ethical responsibility. Today's leaders are expected to not only pursue profitability but to do so responsibly. Sustainable leadership involves making decisions that account for the environmental, social, and economic impacts of business activities. This approach ensures compliance with global standards but also drives innovation in product and service development to cater to the growing demographic of environmentally and socially conscious consumers. Effective leaders incorporate sustainability as a core strategic objective of the organization, demonstrating that profitability and responsibility can coexist to foster long-term business viability and success.

1.2 The Psychological Impact of Leadership Styles on Employee Performance

Well-being:

Leadership style dramatically impacts employee psychological wellbeing beyond operational oversight - affecting stress, job satisfaction, and mental health. An authoritarian style ensuring efficiency often breeds high employee stress through rigid rules and limited input, stifling creativity while leaving employees undervalued and disempowered. Conversely, a democratic style encouraging participation and valuing input boosts satisfaction and well-being by fostering ownership and belonging.

Motivation:

Motivational strategies also psychologically impact the organization. Understanding motivation theories is crucial for leaders aiming to engage teams effectively. Intrinsic motivators like growth, recognition, and achievement often have long-lasting morale effects than extrinsic rewards like bonuses. Recognizing an achievement taps intrinsic drivers by providing social recognition and accomplishment feelings, enhancing commitment and satisfaction.

Emotional intelligence:

Emotional intelligence comprising empathy, self-awareness, and social skills is pivotal for effective leadership. Emotionally intelligent leaders recognize their own and others' emotions, judiciously managing relationships with empathy. They connect with teams, manage emotions in stressful situations, and resolve conflicts effectively. When a project fails, an emotionally intelligent leader assesses the team's emotional state, provides constructive feedback framing failure as a learning opportunity to prevent demotivation and foster resilience.

Feedback Culture:

Establishing an organizational feedback culture enhances psychological well-being and performance. Effective constructive feedback doesn't just correct behaviors - it motivates and promotes growth, creating open communication where employees feel valued and recognized. Encouraging regular two-way feedback where employees provide leadership/ organizational input fosters transparency and trust, helping to adjust strategies, improve processes, bolster engagement, and involve employees in the growth journey.

1.3 Balancing Empathy with Authority: A Key Leadership Skill

Empathy as Strength:

Often narrowly perceived as just a soft skill, empathy is actually a powerful tool for effective leadership, enhancing the authority by fostering an environment of trust and respect. Genuine concern for team members' experiences and feelings builds an essential trust foundation, not weakness. Empathy allows understanding the personal/professional landscapes employees navigate, providing crucial insights for tailored leadership that accounts for team dynamics and individual needs - not diluting the authority but reinforcing precise, caring leadership.

Moreover, empathetic leadership recognizes each team member's unique contribution, appreciating individuality over one-size-fits-all approaches. This nurtures an environment where employees feel valued and understood, encouraging loyalty and effective contributions. Understanding team concerns and aspirations equips leaders to enhance performance and foster a collaborative spirit.

Boundaries:

Empathy plays a key role in setting boundaries too. Respecting personal boundaries and life commitments increases workplace satisfaction and productivity by balancing professional demands against excessive personal time encroachment causing burnout. A leader may respect an employee's family evening commitments or need for flexibility due to personal responsibilities. Thoughtful boundary-setting demonstrates empathy for work-life balance needs while clearly and consistently upholding professional standards.

Difficult Conversations:

Empathy interplays with authority when navigating difficult conversations around performance, conflicts, or changes. An empathetic approach means considering the situation but assertively communicating expectations and realities. When discussing performance issues, an empathetic leader understands potential underlying employee issues, offers support/resources for improvement, but clearly sets required standards and consequences for underperformance - keeping the conversation balanced and productive.

Empathetic leadership impacts broader team dynamics too. Such teams are often more cohesive and supportive, with members feeling secure expressing ideas, sharing concerns, and contributing fully in a supportive environment. This security and mutual respect foster innovation by empowering unique perspectives and enhances collaborative problem-solving. Promoting understanding and collaboration builds productive, innovative, resilient team cultures.

Motivation's Science:

Workplace motivation is a dynamic, complex, psychologicallyrooted phenomenon explaining what propels employees toward goals. Abraham Maslow's hierarchy of needs and Frederick Herzberg's two-factor theory remain highly relevant motivational frameworks.

Maslow's hierarchy posits human actions are motivated by inherent needs ranging from basic physical necessities to higher self-actualization needs. In business, leaders must recognize and address employees' multi-level needs - from ensuring workplace safety to facilitating growth and achievement.

Herzberg's two-factor theory divides motivational elements into "hygiene factors" and "motivators". Hygiene factors like salary and job security don't provide motivation themselves, but their absence breeds dissatisfaction. Motivators like recognition and achievement actively create job satisfaction and motivate excellence. Understanding these allows leaders to design strategies not just preventing dissatisfaction but enhancing engagement and motivation, fostering genuine drive for peak contribution.

While theories provide a useful framework, practical application necessitates a personalized approach considering each team member's unique values, goals and preferences. Personalized strategies involve nuanced insight into what motivates individuals, like opportunities for career growth vs. Work-life balance accommodating flexibility.

Leaders can implement personalization through regular one-on-ones understanding employee aspirations and personal situations, demonstrating genuine interest in wellbeing and professional growth for deeper work engagement. Personalizing goals aligns individual and organizational objectives, enhancing motivation while intrinsically linking work to personal development and long-term career plans.

Workplace autonomy critically boosts motivation, innovation and satisfaction. Autonomy empowers employees to shape their environment and approach, fostering ownership and responsibility. For example, allowing developers flexibility in tackling problems or setting hours yields innovative solutions and more productive.

1.4 The Science of Motivation: Understanding What Drives Your Team

Decoding Motivation:

Motivation in the workplace is a complex, dynamic phenomenon deeply rooted in psychological theories that help us understand what propels employees to achieve their goals. Two foundational theories remain particularly relevant to modern leadership: Abraham Maslow's hierarchy of needs and Frederick Herzberg's two-factor theory. Maslow's hierarchy suggests that human actions are motivated by an inherent desire to fulfill a range of needs, from basic physical necessities to higher-order self-actualization needs. In a business context, this implies that leaders must recognize and address multiple levels of employee needs, from ensuring workplace safety to facilitating personal growth and achievement.

Herzberg's two-factor theory, meanwhile, divides motivational elements into 'hygiene factors' and 'motivators'. Hygiene factors, like salary and job security, don't provide motivation in themselves, but their absence can lead to dissatisfaction. Motivators, such as recognition and personal achievement, actively create job satisfaction and effectively motivate employees to excel. They're not just showing up and going through the motions - they're bringing their A-game, their most creative ideas, and intuitive problem-solving skills. When you've got a team of people who are that engaged and driven, there's no limit to what you can achieve together.

Personalization of Motivation:

While motivational theories provide a useful framework, practically applying them requires a personalized approach that considers each team member's unique values, goals, and preferences. Personalized motivation strategies involve a nuanced understanding of what makes each employee tick. For instance, one team member may be motivated by career advancement opportunities, while another finds motivation in flexible work schedules that accommodate work-life balance.

Leaders can implement personalization by conducting regular one-on-one meetings with employees to understand their professional aspirations and personal situations. This individual attention demonstrates genuine interest in each employee's well-being and professional growth, fostering deeper work engagement. Moreover, personalized goalsetting can align individual professional objectives with organizational targets. Maybe Jenna in accounting is a closet stand-up comedian, or Mark in sales has a passion for photography. Your team starts to see that you genuinely care about them as human beings, not just as cogs in the machine. They feel valued, heard, and motivated to bring their whole selves to work.

The Role of Autonomy:

Granting workplace autonomy is another critical factor in boosting motivation, leading to increased innovation and employee satisfaction. Autonomy empowers employees to shape their work environment and methods, fostering a sense of ownership and responsibility. For example, allowing a software developer freedom to choose how to approach a project problem or set their work hours can lead to innovative solutions and a more productive, satisfying work experience.

However, autonomy doesn't mean a lack of leadership or direction. Effective leaders provide clear goals and accountability structures to guide autonomous work. This balance ensures employees understand their boundaries and the expectations within which they have freedom to operate. Autonomy coupled with proper support and clear objectives encourages employees to experiment and take initiative, potentially leading to groundbreaking innovations and a more dynamic workplace.

Recognition and Reward Systems:

Effective recognition and reward systems are pivotal in reinforcing desired behaviors and boosting morale. Such systems should be thoughtfully designed to align with both motivational theories and the organization's strategic goals. Recognition and rewards can vary from formal programs, like employee of the month, to informal practices like public acknowledgment in team meetings or personal notes of appreciation from supervisors.

Rewards shouldn't be limited to monetary benefits. Non-monetary rewards, such as professional development opportunities, additional time off, or even public acknowledgment, can be highly effective. These rewards directly tap into intrinsic motivators by fulfilling higher-order needs, such as esteem and self-actualization, as described in Maslow's hierarchy. Leaders must ensure these systems are perceived as fair and transparent, with clearly defined criteria for what constitutes rewardable performance. This clarity helps prevent feelings of bias or unfairness that could undermine the recognition system's motivational impact.

It's not enough to have a generic employee recognition program that feels disconnected from what really matters to your team. Instead, take the time to clearly define what constitutes rewardable performance in your organization. What are the specific metrics, behaviors, and values that you want to celebrate and reinforce? Make sure these criteria are communicated clearly to everyone on your team. They should have a solid understanding of what they need to do to earn recognition, and how their progress will be measured. This transparency helps create a sense of fairness and empowerment - people know what they're striving for and feel in control of their own success.

Remember to also recognize and celebrate the intangible qualities that make your team members great - their collaboration, their creativity, their positive attitude. When you highlight these softer skills alongside the quantifiable achievements, you send a strong message about the kind of culture and work ethic you value.

"Leadership is not about titles, positions, or flowcharts. It is about one life influencing another."

- John C. Maxwell, American author, speaker, and pastor who has written many books on leadership.

Chapter 2
Leadership Styles Explored

In the vast landscape of leadership, styles vary as widely as the leaders themselves, each bringing a unique blend of attributes and approaches to the table. The effectiveness of a leadership approach hinges largely on how well it aligns with both the leader's personality and the organizational context. This chapter explores one such style—servant leadership—which is distinguished by its focus on the growth and well-being of people and the communities to which they belong.

2.1 Servant Leadership: Putting Your Team First

Principles:

Servant leadership is about shifting the focus from

commanding to caring, from power accumulation to its equitable distribution within the team. This approach is founded on empathy, active listening, and stewardship. Empathy involves genuinely feeling team members' emotional states to forge deeper connections. Active listening means not just hearing words but interpreting the thoughts and emotions behind them, ensuring team members feel truly heard and validated. Stewardship highlights the servant leader's commitment to the growth and well-being of their team and broader community.

Servant Leadership in Practice:

A real-world servant leadership applications can profoundly impact organizations. For example, a tech company struggling with low engagement and high turnover adopted a servant approach focused on personal growth and empowerment, leading to significant improvements. Leaders were trained to provide tools and support for team success instead of gatekeeping, boosting morale, productivity and reducing costly turnover. The company also enjoyed increased innovation as valued, empowered employees contributed more ideas.

Challenges:

Despite benefits, servant leadership faces criticism that its nurturing nature lacks authority and decisiveness, potentially slowing decisions. In highly competitive or crisis situations, the empathetic approach may seem too soft. To address this, servant leaders must balance empathy with effectiveness through clear goals, boundaries and accountability. They must adeptly resolve conflicts while ensuring kindness isn't mistaken for weakness, maintaining team respect and authority.

Measuring the Impact:

Assessing servant leadership effectiveness requires looking beyond traditional metrics to indicators like employee engagement, team cohesion, retention rates and feedback quality. Regular employee surveys on job satisfaction, perceived management support and growth opportunities provide insights into this model's cultural impact. These gauges reveal servant leadership's effect on individual and organizational growth, highlighting benefits and areas for improvement.

When the COVID-19 pandemic forced businesses to shut down, Dan Price, CEO of Gravity Payments, took a 98% pay cut to prevent laying off any of his 200 employees. He also rented out his home to put more cash into the company. Price empowered employees to make their own decisions about working remotely or on-site, prioritizing their safety. He continuously checked in on their wellbeing, providing support and resources. By putting his employees first, making personal sacrifices, and giving them autonomy, Price exemplified the core principles of servant leadership - empathy, stewardship, and an unwavering commitment to serving others.

2.2 The Dynamics of Democratic Leadership in a Corporate Setting

Features:

Implementing the democratic leadership style will demonstrate its ability to harness the collective wisdom and diverse perspectives of the entire team. The foundational idea behind democratic leadership is that every team member has something valuable to contribute, and that the best solutions emerge when all voices are heard. Rather than decisions being handed down from on high, a democratic leader actively seeks input from across the organization, recognizing that great ideas can come from anywhere.

Benefits:

Democratic leadership's architecture rests on the principle that all team members offer valuable insights benefiting from the organization's success. Involving employees tap diverse perspectives for innovative, effective solutions. When exploring new opportunities, a democratic leader gathers cross-functional input, potentially revealing niche markets or creative strategies a centralized process might miss. This includes problem-solving leverages the team's diverse skills and experiences.

Beyond enhanced decision-making, democratic leadership boosts engagement, satisfaction and innovation. When voices are valued, commitment and organizational loyalty rise. This emotional investment drives discretionary effort and innovation. The democratic process instills ownership over decisions, increasing job satisfaction and reducing turnover.

Challenges and Limitations:

Excessive deliberation seeking consensus can delay action, problematic in fast-paced industries or crises requiring swift decisions. Conflicting strong views may also cause gridlock. Clear decision-making process guidelines like time limits and conflict resolution methods are crucial. While consensus is ideal, leaders must sometimes make unilateral decisions to prevent stalling important initiatives.

Case Studies:

Democratic leadership drove transformations across industries. A software company involved developers, marketers and customer service in decisions, improving products through comprehensive insights while boosting productivity and satisfaction with increased team cohesion.

At Menlo Innovations, a software company, employees have an equal say in decisionmaking through their "double-linking" process. Every week, employee representatives from each project team meet to discuss updates, concerns, and ideas. These representatives then take the feedback to their respective teams for further discussion and input. Final decisions get made collectively, ensuring all voices are heard. The founders consciously avoided a top-down hierarchy, instead fostering a culture of open dialogue, active listening, and shared responsibility. This democratic approach empowers employees, builds trust, and drives innovative solutions that everyone has a stake in.

2.3 Authoritarian Leadership: When is it Effective?

Definitions:

The authoritarian leadership style sits on the opposite end of the spectrum from democratic leadership. In this approach, the leader holds all the decision-making power and exerts a high degree of control over the team.

Under authoritarian leadership, the leader sets the direction, establishes the rules, and makes key decisions independently, with little to no input from team members. This top-down style is often characterized by strict policies, rigid processes, and clear expectations for how work should be carried out. Team members are expected to follow orders and adhere to established procedures without question.

Appropriate Contexts:

In environments where rapid response is crucial, such as during a crisis or in high-stakes situations, the efficiency of authoritarian leadership becomes a significant asset. For example, in emergency response operations, such as firefighting or medical emergencies, the need for quick, decisive action leaves little room for debate or consensus. Similarly, industries that are highly regulated, where strict compliance with laws and regulations is required, benefit from an authoritarian approach. This ensures that procedures are followed precisely, reducing the risk of legal issues or safety hazards. In these contexts, the authoritarian leader's ability to command and direct clearly can be instrumental in navigating the complexities and urgencies typical of such environments.

Risks and Pitfalls:

Despite its advantages in specific contexts, authoritarian leadership carries potential risks that can impact team dynamics and overall organizational health. One of the most significant risks is the potential negative impact on team morale. Teams led by authoritarian leaders might experience low levels of autonomy, which can lead to decreased job satisfaction and higher turnover rates. Creativity can also suffer under authoritarian leadership due to the limited opportunity for team members to contribute ideas or challenge processes. This suppression of creative thought can stifle innovation, leaving organizations less competitive and adaptable to changes in the market.

Balancing authority with compassion:

Balance is crucial for leaders who tend to adopt an authoritarian style. One effective strategy is to establish clear and transparent communication about the reasons behind decisions and the specific expectations set for team members. This can help mitigate feelings of exclusion or unfair treatment. While maintaining control over critical decisions, leaders can find areas within the workflow where team members can exercise some degree of autonomy or make decisions. This not only helps to maintain morale but also encourages a sense of ownership and responsibility.

Another approach is to schedule regular feedback sessions, which allow team members to express their thoughts and feelings about the workplace environment. These sessions can provide leaders with valuable insights into team morale and offer a platform for addressing any concerns, thus maintaining an open line of communication.

Authoritarian leaders can benefit from integrating recognition into their leadership practice. Acknowledging the efforts and achievements of team members can significantly boost morale and loyalty, even in a controlled environment. Recognizing that each team member's contribution is valuable to the organization's success can help balance the scales between authority and personal connection, fostering a more harmonious workplace. This recognition should be both public, to give team members the credit they deserve in front of their peers, and personalized, to show genuine appreciation for individual contributions

Assessment:

In practicing authoritarian leadership, it is vital to continuously assess the impact of this style on both the performance and well-being of the team. Leaders should remain vigilant for signs of declining morale or creativity and be prepared to adjust their approach. This might involve relaxing some controls, increasing transparency, or providing more opportunities for team involvement. By maintaining this balance, leaders can ensure that their use of authoritarian leadership remains effective and that its implementation serves the best interests of both the organization and its employees.

Elon Musk, the CEO of Tesla and SpaceX, is known for his authoritarian leadership style. He demands complete control and obedience from his employees, expecting them to work grueling hours and follow his directives without question. Musk has been known to berate and publicly humiliate those who fail to meet his exacting standards or challenge his decisions. While his uncompromising vision and high expectations have driven innovation at his companies, his authoritarian approach has also led to high employee turnover, low morale, and a culture of fear and intimidation. Musk's refusal to solicit or consider input from others exemplifies the controlling and domineering nature of authoritarian leadership.

2.4 Laissez-Faire Leadership: Autonomy and Trust at Play

Understanding Laissez-Faire Leaders:

This French leadership style's essence allows employees freedom to independently handle tasks, fostering ownership driving remarkable outcomes. Laissez-faire leadership centers on profound trust in team members to self-manage responsibilities with minimal oversight. This leadership style's essence allows employees freedom to independently handle tasks, fostering ownership driving remarkable outcomes. However, effectiveness hinges on context - thriving in environments with highly skilled, self-motivated team capable of self-direction. Freedom breeds groundbreaking innovations

Comprehending laissez-faire leadership necessitates an appreciation for the nuances of delegation and the deep trust placed in team members to manage their own responsibilities. The French term "laissez-faire", meaning "let do" or "let go", perfectly captures the essence of this leadership style. Leaders adopting this approach step back, granting team members the freedom to handle their tasks without constant oversight. This style is based on the belief that employees perform optimally when given space to innovate and make decisions independently, nurturing a sense of ownership and responsibility that can drive remarkable results.

Potential Drawbacks:

Risks include under-management, with laissez-faire's handsoff approach causing direction/cohesion issues like misaligned goals, missed deadlines and inconsistent standards. Some may feel unsupported or directionless, decreasing motivation and engagement.

To make laissez-faire leadership effective, set clear expectations and goals from the start, ensuring everyone is on the same page. Schedule regular check-ins to maintain alignment without micromanaging, and provide guidance as needed. Encourage open communication through feedback systems, so you can stay informed and offer support when required. This approach balances autonomy with accountability, enabling your team to thrive while mitigating risks.

Ideal Conditions:

Project management tools, tracking real-time progress are invaluable for monitoring without constant oversight. A culture of mutual leader-team respect and trust is paramount, with leaders demonstrating confidence through significant responsibility delegation and contribution appreciation. This empowerment and respect are fundamental to laissez-faire's success.

However, the effectiveness of laissez-faire leadership is highly dependent on the context in which it is implemented. It flourishes in environments where team members are not only skilled but also highly motivated and capable of self-direction. Industries that thrive on high levels of creativity and innovation, such as tech startups, research labs, and creative agencies, often see significant benefits under laissez-faire leadership. In these settings, professionals like software developers, scientists, and designers typically value the autonomy to explore new ideas and approaches without the restrictions of strict oversight. This freedom can spark groundbreaking innovations and advancements, as individuals can experiment and leverage their expertise without constant interference.

Accountability:

Ensuring accountability within a laissez-faire framework is crucial to mitigate these risks and harness the potential benefits of this leadership style. Leaders must establish clear expectations and performance standards from the outset, providing a solid foundation upon which team members can operate independently. This involves setting specific, measurable, achievable, relevant, and time-bound (SMART) goals that align with the organization's broader objectives.

Regular check-ins can also play a vital role in maintaining alignment and accountability without veering into micromanagement. These sessions provide an opportunity for leaders to offer support and guidance, address potential issues early on, and recognize achievements, which can help keep team members motivated and on track.

Another effective strategy is the implementation of a robust feedback system that encourages open communication between team members and leaders. This system should not only allow but actively encourage employees to share their progress, challenges, and insights. Such transparency ensures that the leader remains informed about each team me

Technology can be a powerful tool in making laissez-faire leadership work effectively. Project management platforms that provide real-time updates and performance tracking allow leaders to monitor progress and ensure everyone is contributing to shared goals without constant direct oversight. These tools create transparency, enabling teams to collaborate independently while staying aligned. Leaders can quickly identify potential roadblocks and proactively offer guidance or resources. By leveraging the right tools, leaders can create high-performing, self-directed teams that work independently while remaining aligned and supported in driving towards ambitious goals.

Respect and Trust:

In implementing laissez-faire leadership, it is also essential to foster a culture of mutual respect and trust. Leaders must demonstrate confidence in the abilities of their team members by delegating significant responsibilities and showing appreciation for their independent contributions. This not only empowers individuals but also builds a strong sense of mutual respect, which is fundamental for the success of laissez-faire leadership. By carefully balancing freedom with strategic support and accountability, leaders can create an environment where autonomy leads to innovation, engagement, and outstanding performance, making laissez-faire leadership a powerful tool in the right conditions.

At a growing tech startup, the CEO took a hands-off, laissez-faire approach to leading the engineering team. He provided minimal direction or oversight, allowing the team to self-organize and make their own decisions about project priorities, deadlines, and how to accomplish their work. While this autonomy was initially empowering, over time the lack of clear leadership and accountability led to missed deadlines, scope creep, and conflicts between team members. Productivity and morale suffered as the team lacked the guidance and support needed to stay aligned and focused on key objectives. The CEO's laissez-faire style ultimately hindered the team's performance and success.

2.5 Charismatic Leadership: The Power of Persuasion and Vision

Characteristics:

Charismatic leadership, frequently characterized by an individual's magnetic ability to attract and influence others, depends on a set of unique qualities that go beyond mere team management skills. At the heart of charismatic leadership are exceptional communication abilities and a compelling vision that can transform and energize an entire organization.

Charismatic leaders possess an innate talent for articulating a clear and engaging vision that not only paints a picture of a promising future but also rallies the workforce towards achieving shared objectives. Their persuasive communication isn't just about speaking eloquently; it's about connecting with people on a deeper emotional level, making each team member feel valued and understood.

Influence on Morale:

The impact of such leadership on team morale and performance can be profound. Teams led by charismatic leaders often experience a surge in enthusiasm and commitment. This type of leadership breeds an environment where team members are more willing to put in extra effort, driven by the infectious passion of their leader. For instance, in a sales team, a charismatic leader could ignite intense motivation by personally connecting with team members, celebrating their individual successes, and continuously reinforcing the team's impact on the company's goals. This approach not only boosts individual performance but can also enhance team cohesion as members unite under a shared vision and leadership.

Dangers:

While the benefits are considerable, the reliance on the leader's personality and personal influence also introduces significant risks. One of the primary dangers is the potential for abuse of power. The persuasive power of charismatic leaders can, if unchecked, lead to decision-making that prioritizes the leader's personal agenda over the team's or organization's best interests. Such dynamic leadership can foster an overdependence on the leader, with the team potentially feeling lost or unmotivated in their absence. This dependency creates a fragile foundation for the organization, as the departure of the leader could lead to a significant drop in team morale and performance.

Sustaining Success:

To mitigate these risks and ensure sustainable success, charismatic leaders must strive to build robust systems and practices that outlast their personal involvement. It's essential for these leaders to cultivate a leadership pipeline within the organization that promotes the development of a broad base of leadership talent, not just a few charismatic leaders. This involves mentoring potential leaders and exposing them to critical aspects of the leadership process, thereby reducing dependency on any single individual.

Embedding the charismatic vision into the organization's culture can help sustain momentum even when the leader is no longer present. This might include establishing clear values and principles that resonate with the leader's vision and ensuring these are integrated into all aspects of organizational operations.

In essence, while charismatic leadership can significantly elevate an organization's performance and morale, it comes with its set of challenges that require careful management. By focusing on developing a strong leadership culture and embedding enduring systems, charismatic leaders can ensure their positive impact continues, fostering an environment of sustained growth and innovation.

Steve Jobs, the co-founder of Apple, was renowned for his charismatic leadership style. He had a unique ability to cast a compelling vision and inspire unwavering loyalty from employees and customers alike. Jobs' passion, confidence, and showmanship captivated audiences during product launches, convincing them of the innovativeness and superiority of Apple's offerings. He instilled a sense of purpose and pride in being part of something extraordinary. Jobs' charisma and ability to articulate a transformative future enabled him to rally people around seemingly impossible goals and drive Apple's phenomenal success and cult-like following. The dynamic and influential nature of charismatic leadership, can uplift both the leaders and the teams they lead.

The exploration of various leadership styles in this chapter underscores the importance that matching a leadership style to the specific needs and culture of an organization can have profound impacts on its success and health. The next chapter will explore how leaders can adjust their approach to meet the evolving needs of their teams and organizations, ensuring resilience and adaptability in an ever-changing business landscape.

"Leadership is the art of giving people a platform for spreading ideas that work."

- Seth Godin, American author and former dot com business executive, known for his writing on marketing, leadership, and spreading ideas.

Chapter 3
Adapting Leadership to Team Dynamics

Imagine you're leading a global team and a cultural misunderstanding halts the discussion. It's a wake-up call - to be effective, you must adapt your approach to your team's diverse cultural tapestry.

In our interconnected world, navigating cultural diversity is a fundamental leadership skill. It means valuing unique perspectives, being attuned to nuances, and creating an environment where everyone feels heard and respected. When you get it right, you unlock your team's full potential, fostering collaboration and innovation that transcends boundaries.

3.1 Cultural Diversity in Teams: Leading with Sensitivity

It starts with valuing each person's unique perspective and experiences, and creating an environment where everyone feels heard and respected. It means being attuned to cultural nuances, communication styles, and working preferences, and adapting your leadership style accordingly.

Enhancing Cultural Differences:

The benefits can only be realized when you foster an environment where these differences are respected and valued. This requires a deep commitment to learning about and understanding the various cultural norms and values that influence your team members' behaviors and attitudes. For instance, while direct communication might be appreciated in some cultures, others might value a more nuanced or indirect approach. Recognizing and respecting these differences is crucial in preventing misunderstandings and building a cohesive team. It involves more than just tolerance; it requires an active effort to understand and appreciate the diverse worldviews and practices of your team members.

Sensitivity Training:

To aid in this understanding, implementing regular cultural sensitivity training for both you and your team can be incredibly beneficial. These training sessions serve not only as educational tools but also as forums for open dialogue, allowing team members to express their cultural views and educate others about their customs and traditions. This proactive approach not only enhances mutual understanding but also deepens interpersonal relationships within the team, fostering a sense of community and collaboration.

The training should cover essential topics such as cultural communication styles, negotiation norms, decision-making processes, and conflict resolution strategies, tailored to the specific cultural composition of your team. By prioritizing cultural sensitivity training, you are sending a clear message that diversity is not just acknowledged but is a valued asset within your organization.

Customized Communication:

To lead effectively across cultures, adapt your communication to your team's preferences. This might mean adjusting your speech, tone, gestures, and communication channels to what works best for them. For instance, some cultures may find email impersonal, while others appreciate its clarity and recordkeeping. By tailoring your approach, you create an environment where everyone can engage and contribute comfortably. Flexible communication is key to building understanding and alignment in diverse teams.

Understanding the appropriate level of formality in your communication, whether in meetings, emails, or one-on-one conversations, can greatly enhance clarity and prevent potential offenses. Leaders who excel in multicultural environments are those who not only recognize these differences but actively adapt their communication strategies to ensure clear and effective exchanges.

Celebrating Diversity:

Finally, celebrating cultural diversity within your team can significantly enhance morale and solidarity. This celebration can take many forms, from acknowledging and participating in cultural holidays to incorporating a variety of cultural traditions into your team's social functions. For instance, organizing a monthly 'international potluck' where team members bring dishes from their native countries can be a delightful and effective way to encourage cultural sharing and bonding.

Similarly, recognizing and discussing significant cultural events during meetings not only educates the team about different cultures but also shows respect and appreciation for those cultures. These celebrations act as powerful team-building activities, reducing barriers and enhancing mutual respect among team members.

Challenges and Opportunities:

Leading a culturally diverse team is both a challenge and an opportunity. It requires a commitment to continuous learning and adaptation, as well as a proactive approach to fostering an inclusive and respectful workplace. By embracing cultural differences, investing in cultural sensitivity training, adapting communication methods, and celebrating diversity, you can harness the full potential of your team's diverse backgrounds. This not only leads to a more harmonious and productive work environment but also sets a standard for leadership excellence in today's globalized business world.

At Uber, Dara Khosrowshahi, the CEO, has made cultural diversity a top priority since taking over in 2017. He appointed Bo Young Lee as the company's first Chief Diversity and Inclusion Officer to drive this initiative. Under their leadership, Uber implemented training programs to mitigate unconscious biases, increased transparency around workforce demographics, and set ambitious goals for recruiting and promoting underrepresented groups. Khosrowshahi also overhauled Uber's values and culture to emphasize inclusivity, respect, and accountability. By taking concrete actions and leading from the top, Uber has made significant strides in building a more culturally diverse workforce and inclusive environment.

3.2 The Generational Mix: Bridging the Gap with Adaptive Leadership

Understanding Generations:

In today's multifaceted workplace, you face the unique challenge of leading teams that span across multiple generations, each bringing its own set of values, work preferences, and communication styles. From the experienced Baby Boomers to the tech-savvy Generation Z, understanding these generational nuances is crucial for fostering a harmonious and productive work environment. Each generation has been shaped by the distinct cultural, economic, and technological landscapes of their formative years, influencing their behaviors and expectations in the workplace.

Baby Boomers, for instance, often value loyalty and a strong work ethic, and are known for their steadfast approach and reliability. Generation X members, having grown up during the advent of personal computing, show a great deal of independence and adaptability, bridging the gap between the old and new school. Millennials, or Generation Y, are marked by their affinity for technology, value for flexibility, and a strong inclination towards meaningful work that offers a sense of purpose. Lastly, Generation Z has entered the workforce with a full immersion in digital technology from a young age, bringing along a preference for instant communication and a knack for multitasking.

Adaptive Techniques:

Navigating these differences requires adaptive leadership techniques that respect and utilize the diverse strengths each generation brings to the table. This means you might have to flex your leadership style and communication methods to better align with the expectations and motivations of different generational cohorts within your team. For example, while you might adopt more formal communication methods and value recognition through tenure and long-term rewards with Baby Boomers, you could engage Millennials and Generation Z with collaborative technologies and opportunities for rapid progression and frequent feedback. This flexibility helps in minimizing misunderstandings and enhances team synergy, making it easier to achieve common goals.

Mentoring:

Cross-generational mentoring is a powerful tool for enhancing team dynamics. By pairing younger and more experienced employees, you create a two-way learning exchange. Seasoned professionals share traditional skills, while fresh perspectives from younger members bring new ideas to the table. These programs not only transfer knowledge but also build mutual respect and understanding, bridging generational gaps within your team.

For instance, a Baby Boomer with extensive experience in strategic client relationships could mentor a Millennial focusing on digital marketing strategies. Conversely, a Gen Z tech whiz could help a Gen X team member streamline processes using new tech tools. These relationships, while enriching professional skills, also dismantle generational stereotypes and build a more cohesive team culture.

Technology:

Leveraging technology effectively can further bridge the generational gap, particularly in enhancing team communication and engagement. Digital tools and platforms like Slack, Asana, or Microsoft Teams can cater to the tech comfort of younger generations while also bringing efficiency and a new learning curve for older team members. Training sessions that help all generations get up to speed with these technologies can demystify their use and show the practical benefits they bring to daily operations.

Additionally, using social media platforms for team projects can engage younger employees while giving older generations insights into new forms of communication and marketing. This not only enhances collaboration but also ensures that all team members feel involved and valued, regardless of their age.

To effectively lead a multigenerational team, understand and embrace the diverse traits and values of each generation. Adapt your leadership approach to create an inclusive environment where every member can flourish. Recognize the unique strengths each generation brings to the table. Harness these differences as assets, not obstacles. This mindset enhances individual and team performance while enriching your organizational culture.

Through thoughtful leadership, ongoing learning, and smart use of technology, you can navigate the complexities of a multigenerational workforce. Transform generational diversity into a powerful advantage for your team and company. By leveraging the talents of all generations, you build a dynamic, resilient organization ready to tackle any challenge.

At L'Oreal, the world's largest cosmetics company, CEO Jean-Paul Agon has championed generational leadership to bridge the gaps between different age groups in the workforce. Aging created "reverse mentoring" programs where younger employees mentor senior leaders on topics like digital technology and social media. He also implemented mixed-age project teams and leadership development programs that bring together employees from different generations. This cross-generational approach facilitates knowledge sharing, fosters understanding between younger and older workers, and prepares the company for smooth leadership succession. Agon's generational leadership initiatives have helped L'Oreal remain innovative and relevant across multiple consumer demographics.

3.3 Remote Leadership: Strategies for the Digital Age

Effective Communication:

Digital leadership is a management approach that focuses on leveraging digital technologies, platforms, and strategies to drive organizational transformation, innovation, and growth, recognizing the critical role that digital capabilities play in shaping business models, customer experiences, and competitive landscapes in today's fast-paced, technology-driven world.

Pros: Digital leadership offers significant advantages. It boosts agility and adaptability by encouraging experimentation, iteration, and ongoing learning. Innovation and disruption flourish through the strategic use of emerging technologies and calculated risks. Data-driven decision-making is enhanced by leveraging analytics tools for deeper insights. Digital leaders create personalized, omnichannel customer journeys that improve engagement and experiences. Moreover, a culture that values digital skills, innovation, and continuous learning helps attract and retain top digital talent. Embracing digital leadership positions organizations for success in the digital age.

Cons: Despite its benefits, digital leadership comes with challenges. Resistance to change from those comfortable with traditional methods can hinder digital adoption. Cybersecurity and data privacy risks demand robust strategies to safeguard sensitive information. There's a danger of overemphasizing technology at the expense of people.

Balancing technological investments with people-centric approaches is crucial. Continuous learning and development are essential to keep pace with rapid technological changes. Digital leadership may also create or worsen digital divides and inequities among employees, customers, or communities. Addressing these disparities requires thoughtful, inclusive strategies. Navigating these challenges is key to realizing the full potential of digital leadership.

Remote Management:

In the ever-evolving landscape of modern business, the shift to remote work has not just been a trend but a necessity, reshaping the way leadership is practiced. The importance of mastering effective virtual communication cannot be overstated. Maintaining clear and consistent communication is the lifeline of remote team operations.

You must consider the different time zones, work schedules, and personal commitments of team members, which necessitate a more dynamic approach to communicate schedules. Regular, scheduled communications, such as daily or weekly check-ins via video calls, can create a rhythm and structure that help in mitigating the feelings of isolation often experienced in remote settings. Additionally, being intentional about your communication style—clear, concise, yet personal—helps in bridging the physical distance, making your team feel connected and informed.

Building Virtual Teams:

In a remote work setting, building team cohesion can be challenging but also presents unique opportunities to strengthen the sense of community. Regular virtual team-building activities play a crucial role in this effort.

For example, scheduling virtual coffee breaks or remote team lunches where work talk is set aside in favor of casual conversations can significantly boost team spirit. Encouraging personal updates and informal chats during these sessions helps team members get to know each other better. These activities shouldn't be viewed as mere recreation but as strategic initiatives that foster a supportive team environment. By prioritizing connection and camaraderie, you create a foundation of trust and belonging that enhances collaboration and performance.

Celebrating team achievements virtually, whether through public acknowledgments during video meetings or through team newsletters, helps in reinforcing a collective identity and a shared sense of purpose. As a leader, your role in actively participating and sometimes leading these informal gatherings is crucial as it shows your commitment to not just the work, but to the people who make the work possible.

Assessment:

Performance management in a remote setting requires a shift from traditional methods. The foundation of effective remote performance management is setting clear expectations that align everyone with the team's goals. Start by creating detailed project documents that outline roles, responsibilities, and deliverables. Establish clear timelines and milestones, so everyone knows what's expected and when. Make performance metrics accessible and transparent, allowing team members to track their own progress.

Regular virtual check-ins are crucial for discussing these expectations, reviewing progress, and adjusting goals as needed. These meetings provide an opportunity for timely feedback and support. You can address potential issues before they escalate and promptly acknowledge good performance. Approach these check-ins as a two-way dialogue. Encourage team members to share their challenges, successes, and ideas for improvement. Listen actively and offer guidance and resources to help them succeed.

Remember, the goal is not just to evaluate performance but to foster growth and development. Use these interactions to coach and mentor your team members, helping them build skills and confidence. By setting clear expectations, maintaining regular communication, and providing meaningful feedback, you create a framework for remote performance management that promotes accountability, engagement, and continuous improvement. This approach ensures that your team stays on track and feels supported, even when working independently.

Leveraging digital tools for performance tracking can also provide real-time data that helps in making informed decisions about project management and team member development. Tools such as Trello for task management or Google Analytics for performance metrics offer transparent, immediate insights into team operations, enabling more dynamic and responsive leadership.

Work-Life Balance:

Supporting a healthy work-life balance for remote workers is another critical aspect of modern leadership. The blurring lines between home and work can lead to burnout if not carefully managed. As a leader, advocating for and respecting boundaries is essential. Encourage your team to establish dedicated workspaces within their homes, to define clear working hours, and to take regular breaks to disconnect from work. Promoting flexibility, where possible, can also contribute significantly to work-life balance, allowing team members to work during hours they feel most productive. It's important to lead by example in this regard; by managing your own work-life balance visibly, you set a precedent and create an environment where such practices are normalized.

Reed Hastings, co-CEO of Netflix, has been a pioneer in digital leadership. He recognized early on the potential of streaming media and led Netflix's transformation from a DVD rental service to a global streaming giant. Hastings fostered a culture of innovation, data-driven decision-making, and rapid experimentation within the company. He empowered teams to leverage technology, user data, and AI to enhance the customer experience and drive growth. Netflix's seamless digital platforms, personalized recommendations, and original content strategy are testaments to Hastings' vision and digital leadership. His ability to disrupt traditional business models and adapt to the digital age has made Netflix an industry leader.

3.4 Crisis Leadership: Steering Your Team Through Turmoil

During the 2011 Tōhoku earthquake and tsunami in Japan, Naomi Hirose, the president of Tokyo Electric Power Company

(TEPCO), demonstrated exceptional crisis leadership. Despite facing an unprecedented nuclear disaster at the Fukushima Daiichi plant, Hirose remained calm and focused. She swiftly mobilized resources, coordinated emergency responses, and provided transparent communication to the public and stakeholders. Hirose took personal responsibility, working tirelessly to manage the crisis and mitigate its impact. Her decisive actions, empathy for those affected, and unwavering commitment to resolving the crisis exemplified strong crisis leadership in the face of adversity.

Preparedness and Resilience:

Effective crisis leadership is essential for navigating complex, unpredictable challenges. It involves making swift decisions, adapting to change, communicating clearly, and maintaining emotional stability to guide organizations through turbulent times.

However, crisis leaders must also manage significant risks, such as increased stress, the potential for hasty decisions, and strain on relationships and reputation. Balancing these challenges is crucial for successful crisis management. By skillfully navigating crises, leaders can help their organizations weather the storm, emerge stronger, and build resilience for future challenges.

In the unpredictable business world, crises are inevitable. Your true leadership is tested in guiding your team through the turmoil. Effective crisis management requires preparedness and resilience. Foster a culture of readiness by developing clear crisis communication plans that outline protocols for various scenarios. These plans should specify communication channels and each team member's roles and responsibilities.

Cultivate a mindset of adaptability and encourage open communication. Empower your team to raise concerns and suggest ideas. Embrace setbacks as learning opportunities. By setting a tone of readiness and resilience, you equip your organization to face crises with confidence and emerge stronger.

Practicing these plans through regular drills ensures that when a crisis strikes, your team is well-versed in the necessary actions. This preparedness minimizes the chaos and instills confidence and security among your team members, knowing they're not navigating the unknown alone.

Empathy:

Leading with empathy during crises is another critical facet of your role.

Recognizing the stress and uncertainty your team members may be facing is essential. This might mean taking time to listen to their concerns, addressing their fears, and providing support to help them stay mentally and emotionally strong. For instance, during a crisis affecting job security, being upfront about potential impacts and discussing plans to ensure the team's welfare can alleviate anxiety.

Empathy involves being sensitive to your team members' varying personal circumstances. Some might be dealing with personal losses or hardships affecting their work performance. Showing genuine concern and flexible in your expectations during such times can foster a supportive work environment where employees feel valued as individuals, not just as job roles.

Ready to Adapt:

Adaptive decision-making is indispensable in crisis situations. Crises are dynamic; what works for one moment may become obsolete the next. As such, your decision-making must be agile, ready to pivot strategies as situations evolve. This requires a keen eye on unfolding events and an open mind to consider unconventional solutions. It's about balancing swift decisions to mitigate immediate damage with taking time to gather enough information for informed choices.

Encouraging a culture where team members can offer real-time insights and feedback can be invaluable. By fostering this collaborative approach, you tap into a wide range of perspectives and expertise, enhancing your decision-making process. Moreover, this inclusivity in decision-making can also increase your team's commitment to executing crisis strategies, as they feel a sense of ownership and responsibility for the outcomes.

Post-Crisis:

Finally, the post-crisis phase should not be overlooked. Once the immediate threat subsides, it's crucial to shift your focus to learning and development. Reflecting on the crisis and reviewing your team's response can provide critical insights that strengthen your team's resilience and preparedness for future challenges. This involves conducting debriefing sessions to discuss what worked, what didn't, and how to improve.

Reflecting on a crisis serves as a valuable learning opportunity, contributing to a proactive, resilient team culture. Encourage your team to share their experiences and lessons learned. This post-crisis reflection turns challenges into stepping stones, gradually fortifying your team's ability to handle future crises with greater skill and confidence.

3.5 Feedback Loops: Encouraging Open Communication

At Pixar Animation Studios, president Ed Catmull institutionalized feedback loops as a core part of the creative process and company culture. He established regular "BrainTrust" meetings where filmmakers get candid feedback from colleagues on worksin-progress. Pixar leaders encourage error-reporting and "postmortems" after every project to analyze what went well and what could be improved. This open and constant flow of feedback allows for course-correction, knowledge-sharing, and continuous improvement. Catmull's feedback loop leadership approach has fostered a collaborative environment where even the most experienced professionals remain humble learners. It's a key driver behind Pixar's prolific innovation and creative excellence.

Feedback Culture:

To create a strong feedback culture, encourage open communication and continuous improvement through regular feedback sessions across all levels. Structure these sessions to ensure everyone feels comfortable sharing insights, regardless of their position. Consider adding anonymous feedback channels to capture honest, constructive feedback without fear of repercussions. This is especially valuable for sensitive topics or critiques of current processes or leadership.

Demonstrate genuine openness to receiving and acting on feedback. This commitment to transparency and growth is key. Regularly review and analyze feedback to identify trends and areas for improvement. Share these insights and your action plans with the team to show the impact of their feedback.

Celebrate successes and learning opportunities that come from feedback. Recognizing the value of everyone's contributions reinforces the importance of open communication. By creating safe spaces for feedback, demonstrating responsiveness, and highlighting its impact, you cultivate a culture where continuous improvement is the norm and every voice is valued.

Techniques:

Giving and receiving constructive feedback is a skill that requires thoughtful application. When offering feedback, focus on specific behaviors or outcomes rather than the individual. This approach minimizes defensiveness and frames feedback as an opportunity for professional growth. For example, if a project fell short, discuss specific stages of execution that could be improved instead of attributing failure to the team's abilities. This keeps the conversation objective and solution-oriented.

When receiving feedback, model receptiveness and a positive attitude towards growth. Encourage leaders to actively seek feedback and respond with openness and a commitment to act on insights. This approach enhances leadership development and sets a powerful example for the team. By demonstrating that feedback is valued and acted upon, leaders create a culture where continuous improvement is the norm. When everyone sees feedback as a tool for growth, it becomes easier to have honest, productive conversations that drive individual and organizational success.

Remember, the goal of feedback is not to criticize but to collaboratively identify areas for improvement and celebrate successes. By approaching feedback with empathy, specificity, and a growth mindset, you create a powerful catalyst for positive change at all levels of your organization.

Act On It:

Acting on the feedback you receive is where true growth occurs. It's not enough to collect feedback; you must also show that it leads to real changes. Whether adjusting a project plan, revising a communication strategy, or altering a leadership approach, your actions in response to feedback should be visible and communicated back to your team. This follow-through demonstrates that you value their input and are committed to making improvements based on their suggestions.

If feedback indicates meetings are too frequent and disruptive, experimenting with a revised meeting schedule and assessing team satisfaction can show responsiveness to team needs. This responsiveness improves operational effectiveness and strengthens trust and morale.

Continuous Improvement:

Feedback loops are game-changers when it comes to continuous improvement for your team. Take project retrospectives, for example. After wrapping up a big project, get everyone together to chat about what worked well and what could be better next time. It's like a structured way to learn from each experience and make sure those lessons stick. You take those insights and loop them right back into planning and executing future projects. It's like a never-ending cycle of improvement that keeps your team constantly learning and growing together.

And when you make feedback loops a regular part of how your organization works, it's like hitting the communication and growth jackpot. People start talking more openly, they're excited to develop their skills, and everyone's always looking for ways to make things better. All of this feeds right into your big-picture goals. Your team becomes this unstoppable force that's always adapting, evolving, and crushing it. And that's the kind of resilient, forward-thinking team that can take on anything!

3.6 Working with Volunteers

During the COVID-19 pandemic, José Andrés, a celebrated chef and founder of World Central Kitchen, demonstrated exceptional volunteer leadership. He quickly mobilized a global team of volunteer chefs and support staff to provide fresh meals to those in need. Andrés led efforts to set up emergency food relief kitchens in disaster zones, distributing over 60 million meals worldwide. His passion, tireless work ethic, and ability to inspire thousands of volunteers were instrumental to the mission's success. Andrés exemplified servant leadership, putting the needs of vulnerable communities first, empowering his team, and using his platform to rally support for this humanitarian cause.

Leading volunteers and leading employees require different approaches due to the distinct motivations, expectations, and dynamics involved. Here are some key differences between leading volunteers and leading employees:

Motivation:

Employees are primarily motivated by financial compensation, career advancement opportunities, and job security. Leaders can leverage these extrinsic motivators to drive performance and align behavior with organizational goals. In contrast, volunteers are typically driven by intrinsic factors such as a sense of purpose, personal fulfillment, and a desire to contribute to a cause they care about. Leaders of volunteers must tap into these intrinsic motivations and create a compelling vision that resonates with their values and interests.

Accountability:

Employees are bound by employment contracts and job descriptions, which give leaders formal authority and the ability to hold them accountable for specific tasks and outcomes. Leaders can use this authority to set expectations, provide direction, and enforce consequences. With volunteers, however, leaders lack this formal authority and must rely on influence, inspiration, and building a sense of shared responsibility and commitment to the cause.

Retention and Turnover:

When it comes to volunteers, the retention game looks a little different. Volunteers are often giving their time and energy based on personal passion and commitment, rather than a paycheck. While it's still important to keep them engaged and inspired, leaders have to be prepared for a bit more ebb and flow in terms of who's showing up and when. This also means that leaders of volunteers need to be particularly skilled at accommodating different schedules and availability. They can't just plug people into a set schedule and expect them to stick to it like clockwork. Instead, they need to be flexible and creative in finding ways to balance the needs of the organization with the realities of their volunteers' lives.

While managing volunteers may come with some unique challenges, it also offers some incredible opportunities. When people are giving their time and talent purely out of passion and dedication, the energy and enthusiasm they bring can be truly infectious. A skilled leader can harness that energy and use it to create real magic. So, if you're leading a team of volunteers, embrace the differences and lean into the strengths. Be ready to inspire, accommodate, and roll with the punches. And most importantly, never forget the incredible power of a team that's fueled by pure heart and soul.

Training and development:

With volunteers, training and development may be more informal and focused on equipping them with the specific skills and knowledge needed for their roles. Leaders of volunteers must be creative and resourceful in providing training and development opportunities within limited budgets and resources.

The strategies and approaches must be tailored to the unique dynamics and motivations of volunteers versus employees. Successful leaders understand these differences and adapt their leadership styles accordingly to foster engagement, productivity, and ultimately achieve their organizational objectives.

"The task of the leader is to get their people from where they are to where they have not been."

- Henry Kissinger, American politician, diplomat, and geopolitical consultant who served as U.S. Secretary of State and National Security Advisor

Chapter 4
Building and Sustaining High-Performance Teams

In today's ever-changing world, true leadership goes beyond managing resources; it's about building resilient, high-performing teams that can tackle any challenge. Picture two companies with comparable resources embarking on the same project – one triumphs, the other struggles. The key difference? Leadership's approach to fostering team dynamics and setting clear, actionable goals. This chapter explores strategies that transform ordinary groups into extraordinary teams, starting with the crucial foundation of setting transparent, inclusive goals and expectations.

4.1 Setting Clear Goals and Expectations in a Transparent Manner

During the 2011 Tōhoku earthquake and tsunami in Japan, Naomi Hirose, the president of Tokyo Electric Power Company (TEPCO), demonstrated exceptional crisis leadership. Despite facing an unprecedented nuclear disaster at the Fukushima Daiichi plant, Hirose remained calm and focused. She swiftly mobilized resources, coordinated emergency responses, and provided transparent communication to the public and stakeholders. Hirose took personal responsibility, working tirelessly to manage the crisis and mitigate its impact. Her decisive actions, empathy for those affected, and unwavering commitment to resolving the crisis exemplified strong crisis leadership in the face of adversity.

The Importance of Clarity:

Clarity in setting goals and expectations is not just about outlining what needs to be achieved but also about aligning these objectives with the broader vision of the organization. This alignment ensures that every team member is not just aware of what they are working towards but also understands how their contributions fit into the larger picture. For instance, when a team understands that their project on improving customer service interfaces directly boosts customer satisfaction and retention, it enhances their commitment and motivation to achieve the set goals.

Clear, measurable goals act as benchmarks that guide daily activities and decision-making processes, providing a focused roadmap to success. When goals are ambiguous, it can lead to confusion and misaligned efforts, which not only dampen morale but also impede productivity. Therefore, as a leader, it is imperative to articulate goals that are Specific, Measurable, Achievable, Relevant, and Time-bound (SMART), ensuring they are understood and embraced by the entire team.

Transparency in Goal Setting:

Transparency in the goal-setting process fosters trust and inclusivity within the team. Engaging team members in this process not only democratizes it but also leverages the diverse insights and expertise present. This involvement can lead to more robust and achievable goals, as team members contribute perspectives that might not be apparent at the leadership level.

When team members participate in setting goals, they are more likely to take ownership, driving efforts towards achieving them. For instance, when implementing new technology, involving IT staff, end-users, and support teams in setting timelines and milestones ensures goals are realistic and account for potential challenges, enhancing the likelihood of successful implementation.

By being transparent and inclusive in goal-setting, leaders build trust, harness collective wisdom, and foster a sense of shared purpose crucial for extraordinary team performance.

Regular Progress Reviews:

Maintaining momentum and ensuring goals are achieved requires implementing regular progress reviews. These reviews serve as critical checkpoints where the team can assess accomplishments, identify deviations from the plan, and make necessary adjustments.

Regular feedback during these reviews is vital for addressing issues before they escalate. For example, bi-weekly review meetings for a project provide ongoing insights into each phase's progress, allowing for timely interventions to keep the project aligned with its timeline and objectives. These meetings should not only evaluate progress but also provide constructive feedback and support to help the team navigate challenges.

By conducting transparent progress reviews, leaders reinforce accountability, foster continuous improvement, and empower teams to course-correct as needed, ultimately increasing the chances of achieving ambitious goals through strategic adjustments and maintaining focus on priorities. These regular checkpoints are essential for keeping extraordinary teams on track towards realizing their full potential.

Celebrating Achievements:

Celebrating achievements, both major milestones and smaller wins, plays a pivotal role in sustaining motivation and reinforcing a positive team culture. These recognitions serve as affirmations of the team's hard work and success, boosting morale and encouraging continued excellence.

After successfully completing a major project phase, organizing a team lunch to celebrate the milestone can significantly lift spirits and strengthen commitment. Celebrating a team member's effort during a meeting or making company-wide announcements for major accomplishments are other powerful ways to recognize achievements.

Such celebrations not only acknowledge past successes but also inspire the team for future challenges. They reinforce the sense of shared purpose and foster an environment where excellence is celebrated and encouraged. By making celebrations an integral part of their approach, leaders can sustain high performance by continually fueling the team's motivation and reinforcing a culture of achievement.

4.2 Recognizing and Utilizing the Strengths of Each Team Member

Gregg Popovich, is the head coach of the San Antonio Spurs basketball team. Popovich is widely regarded as one of the greatest coaches in NBA history, having led the Spurs to five NBA championships and 22 consecutive playoff appearances. His success as a coach is often attributed to his ability to recognize and utilize the unique strengths of each player on his team.

One of the ways Popovich does this is by tailoring his coaching style and game strategy to the individual talents and abilities of his players. Rather than trying to force players to fit into a predetermined system, Popovich adapts his approach to maximize the strengths of each player and put them in the best position to succeed. He has a keen eye for identifying the unique strengths and talents of each player, and he works closely with them to help them refine their skills and build their confidence.

Off the court, Popovich creates a culture of trust and respect within the Spurs organization. He encourages open communication and feedback, and he empowers his assistant coaches and support staff to take on leadership roles and contribute their own ideas and perspectives. By recognizing and utilizing the strengths of each team member, both on and off the court, Gregg Popovich has built a dynasty in San Antonio that has sustained success over more than two decades. His leadership style demonstrates the power of adapting to the unique talents and abilities of each individual, and creating a culture where everyone feels valued and empowered to contribute their best.

In the realm of effective leadership, understanding and leveraging the unique strengths of each team member is not merely an advantage—it's a fundamental strategy that can significantly amplify the effectiveness and satisfaction of your entire team. This approach, known as strengths-based leadership, focuses on maximizing the natural talents and abilities of individuals rather than spending disproportionate time on correcting weaknesses.

Imagine a scenario where a team member, who has a knack for critical thinking and analytics, is consistently assigned tasks that require high levels of interpersonal communication, which they find challenging. The likely result is a frustrated employee and suboptimal outcomes. However, if you align tasks with each individual's inherent strengths, not only do you enhance productivity, but you also foster a work environment where team members feel valued and understood.

Strengths-Based Leadership:

Imagine a team where each member feels empowered to shine in their unique way. This is the essence of strengths-based leadership – an approach that starts by truly understanding the natural talents and strengths that each individual brings to the table. Rather than solely focusing on improving weaknesses, it's about nurturing and developing those innate strengths.

This mindset shift creates a dynamic environment where people thrive. Susan might be a creative visionary, always sparking innovative ideas. Michael, on the other hand, could be a master organizer, keeping projects running like a well-oiled machine. By leaning into their respective fortes, they become an unstoppable duo – Susan's creativity fueled by Michael's execution prowess.

When you empower people to contribute from their areas of strength, individual performance soars. But the real magic happens with the team synergy – members seamlessly complement each other's capabilities, driving collective success further than any one person could alone. It's about harnessing the full potential of your team's strengths mosaic for extraordinary results.

Personalized Role Design:

Imagine a workplace where every person feels empowered to shine in their unique way. This is the power of strengths-based leadership – an approach that starts by truly understanding the natural talents and strengths each individual brings to the team. Rather than solely focusing on improving weaknesses, it's about nurturing and developing those innate strengths.

This mindset shift creates a dynamic environment where people thrive. Perhaps Sarah is a creative visionary, always sparking innovative ideas. Michael, on the other hand, could be a master organizer, keeping projects running smoothly. By leaning into their respective fortes, they become an unstoppable duo – Sarah's creativity fueled by Michael's execution prowess.

When you empower people to contribute from their areas of strength, individual performance soars. But the real magic happens with the team synergy – members seamlessly complement each other's capabilities, driving collective success further than any one person could alone. It's about harnessing the full potential of your team's unique strengths for extraordinary results.

The next step is to thoughtfully design roles that align with those identified strengths - a practice known as personalized role design. This doesn't mean creating entirely new positions, but rather adapting existing roles to better fit each person's talents. For instance, if Sarah excels in client relations, you could adjust her role to focus more on client-facing activities while reallocating some of her other tasks.

The key is crafting these personalized roles with intention, continually refining them as strengths are identified over time. It's a powerful driver of individual fulfillment and team synergy - allowing each person's talents to take center stage for extraordinary outcomes.

Feedback:

Feedback should be constructive, focusing on what was achieved, what could be improved, and how it can be improved. This approach not only helps in personal and professional development but also enhances the overall quality of work. Treating mistakes as learning opportunities rather than failures fosters a positive learning environment. This learning-oriented approach encourages team members to take calculated risks and innovate, knowing that the focus is on growth and continuous improvement rather than fault-finding.

4.3 The Art of Delegation: Empowerment without Abdication

Anne Sweeney, the former co-chair of Disney Media Networks and president of Disney-ABC Television Group, exemplifies the power of delegation in leadership. During her tenure, Sweeney successfully oversaw a wide range of television properties while empowering her teams to take ownership of their work.

Sweeney encouraged creativity and innovation by giving her team the freedom to make decisions and take risks within a clear framework of goals and expectations. She fostered a culture that valued new ideas and experimentation. At the same time, Sweeney maintained a hands-on approach, providing guidance and feedback through regular meetings with team members.

Clear Communication:

Collaboration and communication were key priorities for Sweeney. She actively worked to break down barriers between departments and teams, encouraging teamwork and idea-sharing. Her leadership style balanced empowerment with accountability, as demonstrated in her approach to developing new television shows. While giving her team the freedom to pitch and develop ideas, she set clear expectations around performance metrics. If a show underperformed, Sweeney collaborated with her team to make necessary adjustments.

Empowerment:

By mastering the art of delegation and creating a motivating culture, Anne Sweeney led the Disney-ABC Television Group to great success, building strong teams and driving innovation and growth across the organization.

When delegating tasks, clarity is key. Effective delegation requires articulating the task's importance, success criteria, deadlines, and available resources. This empowers team members by entrusting responsibilities aligned with their strengths and developmental goals. Clear communication fosters ownership and accountability, enabling individuals to thrive while contributing towards collective success.

Avoid Micromanagement:

When delegating tasks, it's crucial to avoid the pitfall of

micromanagement. While the urge to oversee every detail can be strong, especially on high-stakes projects, micromanaging undermines the very trust that effective delegation is built upon. It sends the unintentional message that you doubt your team's capabilities or judgment, which can be hugely demotivating.

Instead, focus on outcomes rather than rigidly controlling processes. Provide the support and resources they need, but then allow autonomy in how they approach their delegated responsibilities. Regular check-ins create accountability while offering opportunities for constructive feedback. Treat any mistakes as learning experiences to facilitate continuous improvement and calculated risk-taking.

This empowering approach builds far more than just task proficiency. It cultivates capability, confidence, engagement, and a spirit of innovation within your team. When you strategically delegate with trust and an outcomes-mindset, you unlock extraordinary potential for growth and impact. Your team members feel valued and motivated to give their absolute best.

4.4 Conflict Resolution: Maintaining Harmony and Productivity

Indra Nooyi, the former CEO and Chairman of PepsiCo, demonstrated exceptional conflict resolution skills during her tenure, maintaining harmony and productivity within her team. When faced with a dispute with a major bottling partner, Nooyi sought a mutually beneficial solution through open communication and negotiation. She listened to the bottler's concerns while advocating for PepsiCo's interests, ultimately reaching a satisfactory agreement for both parties.

Nooyi also navigated public criticism of PepsiCo's products and marketing practices with grace. She engaged in open dialogue with critics and stakeholders, acknowledging their concerns and committing to positive changes. Under her leadership, PepsiCo invested in healthier product lines, reduced sugar and salt content, and adopted more responsible marketing practices.

Within PepsiCo, Nooyi fostered a culture of open communication and collaboration. She held regular town hall meetings, encouraged employees to voice opinions, and remained accessible to her team. When conflicts arose, she emphasized active listening, empathy, and respectful dialogue, focusing on finding solutions rather than placing blame. By approaching conflicts with a solutions-oriented mindset and commitment to open and honest communication, Nooyi maintained harmony and productivity within her team, demonstrating the power of effective conflict resolution in driving success and building strong, resilient organizations.

Proactive and Mediate:

Conflicts within teams are inevitable, but they can be opportunities for growth when handled skillfully. Proactively managing conflicts involves identifying issues early, fostering open communication, and implementing clear resolution protocols. Effective mediation requires impartiality, actively listening to understand root causes, and facilitating win-win solutions through compromise or creative problem-solving. Approached constructively, conflicts can enhance team dynamics and deepen learning.

Building a Resilient Culture:

Building a resilient team culture that views conflicts as growth opportunities is crucial. This involves framing conflicts as a normal and manageable part of working together, celebrating positive outcomes when conflicts are resolved constructively, and encouraging a mindset of continuous improvement.

When teams see conflicts not as threats but as opportunities to learn, grow, and deepen understanding, they become more resilient and cohesive. A culture that normalizes constructive disagreement and prioritizes finding mutually beneficial solutions allows teams to harness conflicts' transformative potential for positive change and innovation.

4.5 The Role of Continuous Learning in Team Development

Sundar Pichai, the CEO of Google and Alphabet Inc., serves as another powerful example of a leader who emphasizes the role of continuous learning in team development. Pichai has been known for fostering a culture of learning and innovation within the organization.

Under Pichai's leadership, Google encourages employees to pursue personal and professional growth through various learning opportunities. The company offers extensive training programs, such as "Googler to Googler" (G2G), where employees teach each other new skills and share knowledge across different domains. Google also provides employees with access to online courses, workshops, and conferences to help them stay updated with the latest industry trends and technologies.

Pichai himself is a strong advocate for continuous learning. He frequently engages with his team members, asking questions and seeking insights to better understand their challenges and perspectives. He also encourages his team to take risks, experiment with new ideas, and learn from their failures.

By prioritizing continuous learning, Pichai has helped maintain Google's position as a leader in innovation and has successfully navigated the company through various challenges, such as the shift towards mobile computing and the increasing importance of artificial intelligence.

Lifelong Learning:

In today's rapidly evolving business landscape, embedding lifelong learning into team objectives is imperative for long-term success and adaptability. A culture of continuous learning enhances skills and fosters adaptability and proactive growth. It involves shifting from annual training to ongoing learning integrated into daily work. Personalized learning plans align individual development with team needs and career aspirations.

Technology facilitates continuous learning through flexible, accessible formats and social learning platforms. Learning from both successes and failures, with a growth mindset, builds resilience and drives improvement. Retrospective reviews provide insights for future enhancements. By prioritizing lifelong learning, personalized plans, technology, and lessons from outcomes, teams cultivate growth, adaptability, and competitiveness in an ever-changing world.

Personalized Plans:

Imagine a workplace where learning is tailored to how each individual best understands and retains knowledge. This is the power of personalized learning plans – a flexible approach that incorporates a diverse range of instructional strategies and resources to cater to different learning styles and preferences.

For some, hands-on project-based learning allows them to tackle real-world challenges and develop practical skills in an immersive way. For others, adaptive technology that adjusts content and pacing based on their performance is ideal for building mastery at their own pace.

And for those who thrive with more personal guidance, one-on-one mentoring provides the targeted support, feedback, and expert insight to accelerate growth. A seasoned pro can model best practices and share hard-won wisdom in their specific areas of expertise.

The key is designing a blended learning journey that fits each individual's unique needs. This personalized approach means no one is forced into a one-size-fits-all mold. It unlocks engagement, motivation, and the ability to absorb new skills and knowledge in the way that resonates most. By empowering people to learn in their optimal way, organizations can cultivate a culture of continuous growth and development that brings out the best in every employee.

Learning From Success and Failure

Learning from both success and failure is essential for personal and professional growth. While it is natural to celebrate successes and feel discouraged by failures, both experiences offer valuable opportunities for learning and development.

Success provides a boost of confidence and validation that our efforts are paying off. By reflecting on the factors that contributed to our achievements, we can identify effective strategies, skills, and mindsets that can be applied to future endeavors. Success also serves as a motivator, inspiring us to set new goals and push ourselves to even greater heights.

Failure teaches us the importance of perseverance and adaptability. It is through our failures that we learn to pick ourselves up, dust ourselves off, and try again with renewed determination. By embracing failure as a natural part of the learning process, we can cultivate a growth mindset that views challenges as opportunities for learning and development.

Ultimately, the key to learning from both success and failure is self-reflection. By taking the time to analyze our experiences, identify patterns, and extract lessons learned, we can continuously improve and grow. By celebrating our successes and embracing our failures, we can develop the skills, knowledge, and resilience needed to achieve our full potential. is absolutely essential for personal and professional growth. While celebrating wins and feeling discouraged by setbacks is natural, both experiences offer invaluable lessons if we approach them with the right mindset.

Success provides a well-deserved confidence boost and validation that our hard work is paying off. By reflecting on what contributed to that achievement, we can identify effective strategies, leverage our strengths, and apply those lessons to future endeavors. Savoring success also motivates us to dream bigger and push ourselves even further.

It is often through failure that we gain the most insightful lessons about ourselves and our capabilities. Setbacks force us to confront weaknesses, re-evaluate approaches, and build resilience. When we analyze what went wrong and seek feedback, we gain clarity on areas needing improvement. This provides an opportunity to develop new strategies for overcoming obstacles.

"A good leader takes a little more than his share of the blame, a little less than his share of the credit."

- Arnold H. Glasow, American businessman and author known for his humorous quotes on business and leadership.

Chapter 5
Personal Development for Leaders

In today's dynamic corporate environment, the most effective leaders are those who continuously evolve and understand their own leadership dynamics. Harness your full potential through self-assessment and continuous personal development. Please refer to the *DCS5 Personality Assessment* to identify personality traits.

5.1 Self-Assessment Tools for Leadership Styles and Impact

Strengths and Areas of Growth:

Anne Mulcahy, the former CEO of Xerox, became CEO in 2001, Xerox was facing significant financial challenges and was on the brink of bankruptcy. To turn the company around, Mulcahy knew she needed to assess her own leadership style and develop a strategy that would be effective in this challenging context.

Mulcahy used various self-assessment tools, including the Lean In Self-Assessment and the Leadership Practices Inventory, to gain insights into her leadership strengths and areas for improvement. Through these assessments, she identified that her natural leadership style was collaborative and focused on empowering others, but she also recognized the need for decisive action and clear communication in a crisis situation.

Based on these insights, Mulcahy adapted her leadership approach to meet the needs of Xerox and its employees:

1. She focused on building a strong, collaborative leadership team and empowering them to make decisions and drive change.
2. She communicated openly and honestly about the challenges facing the company and the steps needed to address them.
3. She made tough decisions, such as reducing the workforce and selling off assets, to stabilize the company's finances.
4. She invested in research and development to drive innovation and position Xerox for long-term success.

Through her self-aware and adaptive leadership approach, Mulcahy was able to successfully turn around Xerox's financial performance and lay the foundation for future growth. She has been widely recognized for her leadership during this challenging period, and her story serves as an example of the power of self-assessment and continuous development for leaders.

Actionable Insights:

In those darkest hours, Anne's self-awareness helped her rally her people through a shared challenge. And ultimately, it allowed her to steer Xerox back into industry leadership. Her example inspires leaders everywhere to regularly pause for self-reflection and adapt their approach based on the ever-evolving needs of their organization and circumstances.

Understanding your leadership style and its impact on your team is crucial for effective management and personal growth. Self-assessment tools like the Myers-Briggs Type Indicator (MBTI), Leadership Practices Inventory (LPI) or the DCS5 Personality Assessment provide insights into your leadership mechanics, strengths, and areas for improvement. Self-awareness is an incredibly valuable starting point, but having an experienced guide can take those insights to powerful new levels. Just as elite athletes hired coaches to sharpen their skills, today's most effective leaders recognize the benefits of enlisting professional coaches or mentors on their own journeys.

Setting clear, achievable goals and tracking progress allows you to measure your development consistently. Seeking input from colleagues provides diverse perspectives that enhance self-reflection. Maintaining a journal helps absorb feedback constructively and form actionable plans. Dedicating time and effort to self-evaluation, monitoring growth, and integrating insights from others demonstrates a genuine commitment to continuous improvement and adaptability.

5.2 Embracing Vulnerability as a Strength

Authenticity:

Embracing vulnerability as a leader is a powerful catalyst for building truly authentic connections and fostering an environment of trust within your team. When leaders are willing to openly share their own challenges, doubts, and uncertainties, it sends a clear signal that it's safe for others to also express themselves freely.

A compelling real-world example of a leader who embraced vulnerability as a strength is Brené Brown, a research professor, author, and speaker. Brown's work focuses on the power of vulnerability, courage, and authenticity in leadership and personal growth.

In her famous TED talk, "The Power of Vulnerability," Brown shared her own journey of coming to terms with her vulnerability as a researcher and as a person. She discussed how her research on shame and empathy led her to confront her own fears and insecurities, ultimately realizing that vulnerability is not a weakness but a source of strength and connection.

Brown's leadership style is rooted in the belief that vulnerability is essential for building trust, fostering innovation, and creating meaningful relationships. She encourages leaders to:

1. Embrace their own vulnerabilities and share them authentically with others
2. Create a safe space for team members to be vulnerable and take risks
3. Cultivate empathy and understand the experiences and emotions of others
4. Lead with courage, even in the face of uncertainty and discomfort

Team Bonding:

Through her work, Brown has inspired countless individuals and organizations to reframe their perception of vulnerability and harness its power for personal and professional growth. Her own willingness to be vulnerable and share her struggles have made her a relatable and influential leader, demonstrating that authenticity and vulnerability can be transformative leadership qualities.

By embracing vulnerability as a strength, leaders like Brené Brown create more human and connected workplaces where employees feel safe to take risks, learn from failures, and bring their whole selves to work. This approach fosters a culture of trust, resilience, and innovation, ultimately leading to more engaged and motivated teams.

Safe Space for Sharing:

Establish clear guidelines and policies by developing and communicating a code of conduct that outlines expectations for respectful behavior, zero tolerance for discrimination, harassment, or intimidation, and procedures for addressing concerns. Encourage open dialogue by allowing employees to voice their opinions, concerns, and ideas without fear of retribution. Actively listen and respond with empathy and understanding.

Ensure that all employees feel valued, respected, and have equal opportunities for growth and advancement. Provide training and education through regular sessions on topics such as unconscious bias, cultural sensitivity, and effective communication to raise awareness and promote a culture of respect.

Leaders and managers should lead by example by modeling the behavior they expect from others, demonstrating respect, empathy, and a willingness to listen and learn from diverse perspectives. Foster a supportive environment by encouraging teamwork, collaboration, and a sense of community. Celebrate successes and support employees through challenging times. By implementing these strategies, businesses can create a safe space where employees feel valued, respected, and empowered to contribute their best work.

Vulnerable Moments

Vulnerable moments in the workplace, such as making a mistake, receiving critical feedback, or experiencing a setback, can be incredibly valuable learning opportunities if approached with the right mindset. The key is to embrace vulnerability as a chance for growth rather than letting it diminish your confidence or make you defensive.

First, acknowledge the vulnerable situation and allow yourself to fully experience the discomfort or disappointment. Don't bury or ignore those feelings. Sitting with the vulnerability helps build resilience. Next, practice self-compassion by avoiding harsh self-criticism. Remind yourself that everyone experiences setbacks and imperfections are part of being human.

With an open mindset, reflect deeply on what occurred and your role in it. Pinpoint areas for improvement and identify the lessons you can extract. Ask others for their perspectives and feedback - vulnerable moments provide keen insights you may have missed. Commit to applying those lessons proactively going forward. Make a tangible plan for how you will respond differently next time. Share your learning experience to help others avoid similar pitfalls. The vulnerability demonstrates humility and courage.

While uncomfortable in the moment, lean into vulnerable situations at work. Approached positively, they provide the opportunity for tremendous personal and professional growth that will compound over time. The most successful leaders are those who can deftly navigate vulnerability.

5.3 Time Management: Leading by Example

Let's consider the example of Arianna Huffington, the co-founder and former editorin-chief of The Huffington Post. Huffington is known for her strong advocacy of worklife balance and the importance of prioritizing well-being in the workplace.

Balance:

In 2007, Huffington experienced a wake-up call when she collapsed from exhaustion, leading her to reevaluate her approach to work and life. She began prioritizing sleep, meditation, and self-care, recognizing that her own well-being was essential for her effectiveness as a leader. Huffington then made it her mission to promote a healthier work-life balance within her organization.

She implemented several initiatives at The Huffington Post, such as:

1. Encouraging employees to take breaks and prioritize their well-being
2. Providing nap rooms in the office for staff to recharge
3. Offering meditation and yoga classes to help manage stress
4. Leading by example and sharing her own experiences with burnout and the importance of self-care

Huffington's leadership style and commitment to work-life balance not only improved the well-being of her employees but also contributed to the success and growth of The Huffington Post. Her approach demonstrated that prioritizing well-being and setting boundaries can lead to increased productivity, creativity, and job satisfaction.

By modeling effective time management and self-care practices, Arianna Huffington inspired her team to adopt healthier habits and created a workplace culture that valued employee well-being. Her example showcases the positive impact that leaders can have when they prioritize work-life balance and lead by example.

Prioritize:

In today's fast-paced world, a leader's time and energy are precious resources. By intentionally prioritizing tasks based on their impact and alignment with strategic objectives, leaders can ensure their efforts are laser-focused on what truly moves the needle. A simple yet powerful tool for this is the Eisenhower Box, which helps categorize tasks into four quadrants based on urgency and importance. This shines a light on the critical priorities deserving immediate attention while identifying lower-impact tasks that can be delegated or deferred.

For leaders, striking this balance between leadership responsibilities and operational tasks is key. It's tempting to get bogged down in the daily fires, but that often comes at the expense of casting the strategic vision and developing their people. This is where the practice of strategic delegation becomes a superpower. By entrusting the right tasks to capable team members, leaders empower growth while freeing up their own bandwidth for higher-level initiatives. It demonstrates trust while providing meaningful development opportunities.

Boundaries:

Maintaining healthy boundaries around work and personal life is crucial for leaders to model. When they respect their own limits and prioritize self-care, it sets a powerful example that prevents burnout and establishes the organization values work-life balance. Team members feel empowered to follow suit, fostering an environment of mutual support. This caring leadership approach nurtures a more sustainable, balanced culture that unlocks the fullest potential in everyone.

Imagine a high-powered executive, Jessica, known for her drive and tireless work ethic. While her results were impressive, the long hours and weekends spent glued to her laptop took a toll. Jessica began to feel rundown and disconnected from the other priorities in her life.

Then one day, Jessica's teenage daughter pointed out that she had missed yet another important family event due to work. It was a wake-up call. Jessica realized that while her dedication was commendable, she was modeling deeply unhealthy norms about what success required.

5.4 Nurturing Emotional Intelligence for Better Leadership

Emotional Intelligence (EI):

Emotional intelligence is a make-or-break quality for today's leaders. It represents a powerful capability to not just manage tasks, but to truly connect with and inspire people. At its core, EI is about self-awareness – having a thoughtful understanding of your own emotions, strengths, weaknesses, and values. It's then using that self-knowledge to take ownership through self-management when situations run high.

Empathy:

Howard Schultz, the former CEO and chairman of Starbucks, provides a compelling example of how nurturing emotional intelligence can lead to better leadership. Schultz has been widely recognized for his leadership style, which prioritizes empathy, compassion, and the well-being of his employees.

Under Schultz's leadership, Starbucks implemented several initiatives that demonstrate his commitment to emotional intelligence. For example, the company provides comprehensive health insurance to all employees, including part-time workers, and offers free college tuition through a partnership with Arizona State University. Schultz believed that by investing in his employees' well-being and personal growth, he could create a more engaged and motivated workforce.

Schultz also emphasized the importance of open communication and active listening. He regularly visited Starbucks stores to engage with employees and customers, seeking to understand their needs and concerns. This approach helped him build strong relationships and foster a sense of trust and loyalty within the organization.

Conflict Resolution:

During times of crisis, such as the 2008 financial recession, Schultz's emotional intelligence was particularly evident. He made tough decisions, such as closing underperforming stores and laying off employees, but he did so with compassion and transparency. He openly communicated with his team, explaining the reasons behind his decisions and offering support to those affected.

By nurturing emotional intelligence, Howard Schultz created a culture at Starbucks that valued empathy, compassion, and open communication. His leadership style not only contributed to the company's financial success but also earned him the respect and admiration of his employees and customers alike. Schultz's example demonstrates that emotionally intelligent leaders can build strong, resilient teams and navigate challenges more effectively.

5.5 The Leader as a Coach: Developing Future Leaders

Jack Welch, the former CEO of General Electric (GE), is another prominent example of a leader who embodied the concept of a leader as a coach, focusing on developing future leaders within his organization. During his tenure at GE from 1981 to 2001, Welch implemented several initiatives aimed at identifying, nurturing, and promoting top talent.

Coaching for Growth:

One of Welch's most notable coaching strategies was the "4E" leadership model, which emphasized the importance of energy, energizing others, edge (the ability to make tough decisions), and execution. He believed that by focusing on these key traits, he could help develop strong, well-rounded leaders who could drive the company's success.

Welch also implemented a rigorous performance evaluation system known as "rank and yank," in which employees were ranked based on their performance, and the bottom 10% were typically let go. While controversial, this system was designed to identify and reward top performers while also providing opportunities for coaching and improvement for those who were struggling.

In addition to these formal programs, Welch was known for his hands-on approach to coaching and mentoring. He would regularly engage with employees at all levels of the organization, offering guidance, feedback, and support to help them develop their skills and advance their careers.

Mentoring vs. Coaching:

One notable example of Welch's coaching leadership style was his role in mentoring Jeff Immelt, who eventually succeeded him as CEO of GE. Welch recognized Immelt's potential and invested significant time in coaching and preparing him for the top leadership role.

While both mentoring and coaching serve distinct purposes at different career stages. Mentoring nurtures long-term, holistic growth through an experienced mentor's guidance encompassing professional and personal domains. It pairs a seasoned professional with a mentee, offering wisdom and support drawn from the mentor's extensive journey. Coaching tends to be more short-term and skill-focused, helping individuals enhance specific competencies. A coaching scenario might concentrate on specific skills like enhancing presentation abilities or mastering a new technology, with defined sessions and expected outcomes agreed upon by both the coach and the team member.

Feedback that Promotes Development:

Delivering feedback that truly facilitates development without demotivating the recipient requires skill and thoughtfulness. Constructive feedback should be timely, specific, and focused on behaviors rather than personal characteristics. For example, instead of saying, "You didn't handle that well," a more constructive approach would be, "I noticed you seemed uncertain during the project meeting. Let's explore how you might approach it differently next time."

Providing feedback is about more than just pointing out areas that need improvement - it's an opportunity to initiate a growth-fostering dialogue. Done well, effective feedback opens up a conversational space to explore development goals and how best to pursue them together.

It's also crucial to counterbalance constructive criticism with genuine positive reinforcement. Taking the time to recognize successes, strengths, and progress goes a long way in building confidence. It reinforces what's working well so those effective behaviors become ingrained habits.

Individual Development Plans:

Imagine a workplace where personal growth isn't just an annual checklist item, but a collaborative, energizing journey tailored to each individual's aspirations. This is the power of effective leadership coaching through customized Individual Development Plans (IDPs).

Creating an IDP begins with an open, engaging dialogue. It's a chance for leaders to truly understand their team members' career goals, natural strengths, and areas they want to develop further. But it's also about aligning those individual ambitions with the organization's overarching vision and needs.

The IDP is a highly personalized roadmap that propels growth in a direction that is mutually beneficial. If someone dreams of leading teams, their IDP might include leadership training, project management opportunities, and cross-department immersion to expand their perspective. Through ongoing coaching conversations, IDPs remain agile and hyper-relevant, capturing new goals and pivoting strategies as needed.

"Leadership is about making others better as a result of your presence and making sure that impact lasts in your absence."

- Sheryl Sandberg, American business executive, billionaire, and philanthropist, currently serving as Chief Operating Officer (COO) of Meta Platforms.

Chapter 6
Fostering a Culture of Innovation and Growth

Innovation is not just about sparking brilliant ideas; it's about cultivating an environment where these ideas can be tested, falter, and evolve without fear. Imagine a world where the light bulb was never invented because Thomas Edison feared failure and gave up after his first few unsuccessful attempts. This analogy underscores a fundamental truth in the business world: fostering an innovative culture necessitates embracing risks and viewing failures as stepping stones to success. This chapter guides you through creating a workspace that not only tolerates but encourages risk-taking and learning from missteps, transforming potential setbacks into powerful catalysts for innovation.

6.1 Encouraging Risk-Taking and Learning from Failure

Sara Blakely, the founder and CEO of Spanx, has built a successful company by embracing risk-taking and learning from her failures. Blakely started Spanx with just $5,000 and a vision for creating innovative undergarments that would make women feel more confident and comfortable.

When she first tried to manufacture her product, she was turned down by multiple factories who didn't see the potential in her idea. Rather than giving up, Blakely persisted and eventually found a manufacturer who was willing to take a chance on her vision.

Blakely has also been open about the failures and mistakes she's made along the way. In interviews, she has talked about the importance of embracing failure as a learning opportunity and using it to inform future decisions and strategies. She has encouraged her employees to take risks and try new things, even if they don't always succeed.

One way that Blakely has fostered a culture of risk-taking and innovation at Spanx is through her hiring practices. She looks for employees who are creative, resourceful, and willing to think outside the box. Blakely has also created a workplace culture that values collaboration, experimentation, and continuous learning. Blakely's approach to risktaking includes her decision to expand Spanx beyond its core product line of undergarments. In recent years, the company has launched new products, such as leggings, activewear, and even men's underwear. While these new product lines were a departure from Spanx's core business, Blakely saw an opportunity to leverage the company's brand and expertise to reach new customers and markets.

By embracing risk-taking and learning from failure, Sara Blakely has built Spanx into a highly successful and innovative company. Her leadership style has inspired her teams to think creatively, embrace challenges, and view setbacks as opportunities for growth and learning. Blakely's example demonstrates the power of persistence, resourcefulness, and a willingness to take calculated risks in pursuit of a vision.

Fostering a Safe Environment for Experimentation:

Fostering a team culture where risk-taking fuels innovation requires boldly challenging traditional risk-aversion. As a leader, you set the tone - communicating that calculated risks are encouraged and that failures leading to growth aren't reprimanded, but celebrated as valuable lessons.

Imagine carving out "innovation time" where your team can fearlessly explore projects beyond their daily responsibilities, without the pressure of immediate perfection. This freedom to experiment creates a safe space for creativity to flourish. When you model an open mindset towards "intelligent failures," you give your team the courage to think big, push boundaries, and embrace the inherent risks that drive true breakthroughs. It's this future-focused culture that unlocks your team's fullest innovative potential.

Google's famous '20% time,' which encourages employees to spend one day a week working on side projects, has led to successful ventures like Gmail and AdSense, illustrating how a safe space for experimentation can yield substantial innovations. Moreover, it's crucial to establish clear parameters that define what constitutes a 'calculated risk'. This involves creating guidelines that help team members make informed decisions about the risks worth taking. These guidelines should include criteria such as potential impact, alignment with business goals, and available resources, ensuring that the risks are thoughtful and not reckless.

By providing a framework for risk-taking, you help your team understand where their creativity lies, encouraging them to explore new ideas while still aligning with the organization's strategic objectives.

The Role of Failure in Innovation:

Change the narrative around failures from being endpoints to being part of a continuous learning journey. Educating your team about the role of failure in innovation through regular discussions, workshops, and real-world case studies can demystify and destigmatize failure.

For example, sharing stories of well-known successes that were born from failure, such as Dyson's 5,126 failed prototypes before successfully creating the bagless vacuum cleaner, can illustrate how perseverance through failure can lead to breakthrough innovations. It is beneficial to implement reflective practices that encourage teams to analyze why an idea failed and how these lessons can inform future projects.

This can be facilitated through 'failure post-mortems'—structured reviews of what went wrong, what was learned, and how these lessons can be applied moving forward. These sessions should be blame-free and focused solely on extracting insights, ensuring that they are constructive and truly beneficial.

Celebrating Attempts, Not Just Successes:

These celebrations, whether public ceremonies at company meetings or creative team rituals, send a powerful message: We value the journey of innovation as much as the destination. They reinforce that taking calculated risks to pursue breakthroughs is not only accepted here, but fundamentally respected and encouraged.

When creative ingenuity is visibly applauded, it gives every team member permission to step out of their comfort zones. It inspires more bold thinking and experimentation. People feel safe to aim high, emboldened by a culture that celebrates their courage as much as their achievements.

Learning and Adapting from Missteps:

In today's rapidly changing landscape, the most future-proof organizations are those that can nimbly adapt when the unexpected arises. Developing this organizational resilience requires cultivating a growth mindset at every level. It's the openness to embrace missteps, quickly assimilate their insights, and iterate with that newfound wisdom. Rather than rigid adherence to initial plans, it's maintaining flexibility to rapidly course-correct strategies and approaches based on real world feedback.

By building in creative reassessment loops, teams can smoothly pivot and enhance their approach with every "unsuccessful" outcome along the way. Each failure becomes a conscious step towards the ultimate solution. This makes an organization exponentially more responsive and inventive. When teams feel empowered to learn and evolve through missteps, innovation flows more fluidly. The fear of failure dissipates, allowing people to take intelligent risks. Setbacks are reframed as opportunities versus roadblocks.

6.2 The Importance of Vision Casting in Inspiring Innovation

Yvon Chouinard, the founder and former CEO of Patagonia, is

a powerful example of a leader who used vision casting to inspire innovation and create a purpose-driven company. From the beginning, Chouinard had a vision for Patagonia that went beyond just selling outdoor clothing and gear. He wanted to create a company that was environmentally responsible, socially conscious, and committed to using business as a force for good.

Chouinard embedded sustainability and social responsibility into every aspect of Patagonia's business model. He sourced materials from ethical and environmentally friendly suppliers, donated a portion of the company's profits to environmental causes, and encouraged customers to buy only what they needed and repair their clothing instead of replacing it.

Chouinard also had a vision for creating a workplace culture that valued work-life balance, creativity, and innovation. He instituted policies like flexible work schedules, on-site childcare, and paid time off for employees to volunteer in their communities. He believed that by taking care of his employees and creating a positive work environment, he could inspire them to bring their best ideas and energy to their work. Under his leadership, Patagonia became known as a leader in corporate social responsibility and a model for how businesses could prioritize people and the planet alongside profit.

Creating and Communicating a Compelling Vision:

A clear vision that genuinely moves people in this way has the power to unite and rally an entire organization. It gives permission and inspiration to think bigger, embrace risks, and relentlessly innovate beyond current constraints. That emotional energy and drive for groundbreaking progress is what can ultimately propel an organization to achieve the extraordinary.

Crafting such a vision demands a deep understanding of your business's core capabilities, market opportunities, and the aspirations of your team. It involves projecting forward into the future, imagining not just where your industry is headed, but where you want to lead it.

To start, work with different stakeholders like leaders, employees, and customers to gather insights and perspectives. This collaborative approach makes the vision inclusive and relevant to everyone in the organization. The real challenge is communicating the vision clearly and simply, so it becomes a shared goal that everyone understands, regardless of their role. Regular discussions, workshops, and storytelling can help reinforce the vision, making it part of the organization's culture and daily work.

Aligning Team Efforts with Vision:

The true power of a well-crafted vision is realized only when the efforts of every team member are aligned with it. Leaders must break down this overarching vision into specific, actionable objectives that teams and individuals can work towards. For instance, if the vision is to become the leader in sustainable practices within your industry, departments should translate this into specific projects like reducing waste, optimizing energy use, or sustainable sourcing of materials. Each team member should understand how their role impacts these targets.

Aligning incentives and rewards with these objectives can motivate teams to consistently aim towards fulfilling the larger vision, reinforcing their commitment and accountability to the organizational goals.

Storytelling in Vision Casting:

Storytelling is one of the most powerful tools at your disposal when it comes to embedding a vision within the company culture. A well-told story can illuminate the vision, providing context and emotional connection that plain statements cannot. It transforms the vision from an abstract concept into a relatable, inspiring narrative. Leaders should craft stories that embody the vision, showcasing potential futures that engage and excite the team.

These stories might include scenarios of how products could change lives, how the workplace culture could evolve, or how the business could impact the world. For example, instead of merely stating a goal to enhance customer satisfaction, share a future scenario where a customer's feedback leads directly to a product modification that dramatically increases its usability and market appeal.

This not only illustrates the commitment to customer-centric innovation but also makes the impact of such a vision tangible to the team. Regularly sharing such stories in meetings, newsletters, or corporate events can keep the team connected to the vision, making it a living part of your organizational narrative.

Revisiting and Revising the Vision:

The business landscape is continuously evolving, influenced by changes in technology, consumer preferences, and global markets. As such, a static vision can quickly become outdated, losing its relevance and effectiveness. It is crucial, therefore, to periodically revisit and potentially revise your vision to ensure it remains aligned with the current business environment and future opportunities.

This should not be seen as an admission of poor planning, but rather as an agile response to a dynamic world, demonstrating flexibility and foresight in leadership. During these sessions, evaluate if the vision still inspires, if it aligns with the current capabilities and market conditions, and if it continues to guide decision-making effectively.

If discrepancies arise, adjustments should be made, whether they involve refining the vision to better capture emerging opportunities or redefining it to address unforeseen challenges. These revisions should then be communicated back to the team with the same clarity and enthusiasm as the original vision, ensuring the entire organization continues to move forward with a unified, relevant, and motivational purpose.

6.3 Leveraging Diversity for Creative Problem Solving

Reshma Saujani, the founder and CEO of Girls Who Code, is an excellent example of a leader who leverages diversity for creative problem solving. Saujani founded Girls Who Code in 2012 with the mission of closing the gender gap in technology and changing the image of what a programmer looks like and does.

To achieve this mission, Saujani knew that she needed to bring together a diverse group of perspectives and experiences. She recruited a team of women from a variety of backgrounds, including educators, technologists, and business leaders, to help design and implement the Girls Who Code curriculum and programs.

Saujani also partnered with companies like AT&T, Google, and Twitter to provide girls from underrepresented backgrounds with opportunities to learn coding skills and gain exposure to careers in technology. By bringing together girls from diverse socioeconomic, racial, and ethnic backgrounds, Saujani created a learning environment where students could share their unique perspectives and ideas, and work together to solve problems in creative ways.

Under Saujani's leadership, Girls Who Code has grown into a global movement, reaching over 300,000 girls in all 50 U.S. states and around the world. The organization has also inspired countless other initiatives aimed at increasing diversity and inclusion in the tech industry.

Value of Diverse Perspectives:

Saujani's example demonstrates the power of leveraging diversity for creative problem solving. By bringing together people from different backgrounds and experiences, leaders can create an environment where new ideas can flourish and innovative solutions can emerge. This approach not only leads to better outcomes, but also helps to build a more inclusive and equitable society.

In today's modern business landscape, where challenges are as varied as the global market itself, the ability to innovate through a variety of perspectives is invaluable. Diverse teams inherently bring a rich tapestry of backgrounds, experiences, and ways of thinking that can greatly enhance the creative problem-solving process. When individuals from different cultures, genders, age groups, and professional disciplines come together to address a problem, they each contribute unique viewpoints that can challenge conventional wisdom and inspire innovative solutions.

Inclusivity:

This diversity creates a breeding ground for creativity where the synthesis of different ideas can lead to breakthroughs that might elude more homogenous teams. For example, consider a tech company that integrates artists and psychologists into its development teams to innovate user interfaces. The artists offer an aesthetic perspective while the psychologists provide insights into user behavior, resulting in a product that is not only functional but also engaging and intuitive.

The key here is to recognize and utilize these diverse perspectives in a way that they complement each other, turning potential conflicts into opportunities for innovation. These practices ensure that all team members, regardless of their background or role, feel valued and empowered to contribute their best ideas.

Unconscious Bias:

Unconscious Bias can subtly influence perceptions and interactions within the team. These biases, often invisible and unintentional, can lead to preferences for certain types of ideas or people, thus stifling diversity's potential to enhance innovation. To combat this, it is crucial to first acknowledge that everyone has biases and that they can distort the way we perceive and evaluate others.

We all carry biases - those unconscious lenses shaped by our experiences that can inadvertently introduce blind spots. As leaders, uncovering and mitigating these hidden biases is essential for cultivating truly innovative, inclusive team environments. Imagine training sessions that go beyond dry compliance, but create a safe space for powerful self-discovery. Through eye-opening workshops exploring cultural impacts or tools like the Implicit Association Test, people gain new awareness of how their backgrounds have shaped their perspectives, often in surprising ways.

Diverse Teams:

A global consumer goods company's diverse R&D team helped create successful products for a wide range of consumers. The team had members from six countries, different genders, and various backgrounds like engineering, marketing, and anthropology. They were asked to make new personal care products. By combining insights from different cultures and fields, the team made a very successful product line that met local preferences and global trends, leading to significant growth in market share.

When we capitalize on our collective cognitive diversity, our ideas become more nuanced, inventive, and engineered for positive impact across more audiences As you continue to build and nurture this diverse and inclusive environment, remember that each varied perspective adds a unique strand to the rich tapestry of your team's collective creativity, propelling your organization forward in a competitive and ever-changing business landscape.

6.4 Creating Spaces for Collaboration and Co-creation

Collaborative Workspaces: In physical spaces, this might involve creating open floor plans where informal meeting areas are abundant and easily accessible. These areas, equipped with comfortable seating and devoid of barriers, encourage spontaneous discussions and brainstorming sessions. Whiteboards and glass walls can invite team members to jot down ideas and collaborate visually, which can be particularly helpful during brainstorming sessions.

Sessions:

In the digital world, the virtual workspace should also support collaboration. This means using platforms that let team members communicate and share files easily. These tools should also be easy to use and inclusive, working for team members with different levels of tech skills. This way, everyone can fully participate no matter where they are or how much they know about technology.

Running good brainstorming and collaboration sessions is both an art and a science. It begins with setting clear goals for each session and telling all participants about them ahead of time. This preparation lets team members collect their thoughts and come to the session with ideas and suggestions, ready to participate fully. Techniques like saying "yes, and..." to build on each other's ideas instead of rejecting them can create a more inclusive and productive brainstorming environment. Also, having a facilitator to guide the discussion, make sure everyone is heard, and keep the session on track can make these collaborations much more effective.

Building a Culture of Co-creation:

Building a culture of co-creation where collaboration is not just encouraged but ingrained involves more than just having the right tools and processes; it requires a shift in mindset and values. This culture is rooted in the understanding that everyone has something unique to contribute and that the best ideas often come from the synthesis of diverse perspectives. Encourage practices such as rotating leadership in meetings, where different team members take turns facilitating brainstorming sessions or leading projects. This not only empowers individuals and gives them a sense of ownership but also brings new perspectives to the forefront, enriching the collaborative process.

Implementing recognition programs that celebrate teams for successful collaborative projects or innovative problem-solving can motivate team members to engage in and prioritize collaborative over solitary work. This recognition should be visible and celebrated across the organization to highlight the importance of collective success and the power of working together.

As this chapter ends, think about how powerful well-designed collaborative spaces and a co-creative culture can be. These things are essential for using the collective intelligence and creativity of your team, pushing your organization towards innovative solutions and continued growth. As you go forward, remember that the spaces we make and the cultures we build play a crucial role in shaping the future of our organizations.

"The greatest leader is not necessarily the one who does the greatest things. He is the one that gets the people to do the greatest things."

- Ronald Reagan, 40th President of the United States, serving from 1981 to 1989.

Chapter 7
Ethics, Integrity, and Transparency

In the high-stakes arenas of modern business, the path you choose to achieve success is as crucial as the achievements themselves. Ethical leadership, a vital but sometimes overlooked cornerstone of effective management, extends far beyond mere compliance with laws and regulations. It shapes the very essence of your organization's character and forms the bedrock upon which lasting trust and respect are built.

Consider the story of a leading tech company that once faced a critical decision about user data handling. The choice was easier access to big data, arguably leading to higher profits, or stringent privacy controls, aligning with ethical standards and customer expectations. The decision to prioritize ethical standards not only enhanced customer trust but also set a new industry benchmark for privacy. This narrative underscores the profound impact ethical leadership has on shaping business practices and public perception.

7.1 Ethical Decision Making: A Guide for Leaders

Arne Sorenson, the former CEO of Marriott International, provides a compelling example of ethical decision making in leadership. In 2018, Marriott was faced a significant data breach that exposed the personal information of over 500 million guests. As soon as the breach was discovered, Sorenson took swift action to address the issue and prioritize the safety and security of Marriott's customers.

Sorenson made the ethical decision to be transparent about the breach and communicate openly with customers about what had happened and what steps Marriott had taken to resolve the issue. He also made the decision to offer free identity theft monitoring services to all affected customers, even though this came at a significant cost to the company.

Throughout the crisis, Sorenson emphasized the importance of taking responsibility for the breach and working to regain the trust of Marriott's customers. He led by example, personally reaching out to customers and stakeholders to apologize for the incident and reaffirm Marriott's commitment to data security.

Sorenson's ethical leadership during the data breach crisis helped to mitigate the damage to Marriott's reputation and maintain the trust of its customers. His actions demonstrated the importance of prioritizing integrity, transparency, and accountability in the face of difficult challenges.

Frameworks for Ethical Decision Making:

Ethical decision-making in today's business landscape demands a well-defined, structured approach. An effective framework starts by identifying the ethical dilemma, assessing the potential outcomes, and examining one's duties and responsibilities. It also involves self-reflection on personal values and integrity, creative problem-solving to find alternative solutions, and trusting one's instincts.

Consider a scenario where you must choose between artificially boosting quarterly results through aggressive accounting tactics or presenting a more modest, but accurate, financial report. By employing this ethical decision-making framework, you can carefully balance the immediate gains against the enduring principles of honesty and transparency that safeguard a company's reputation and ensure adherence to financial regulations.

It's about more than just rules - it's a mindset of integrity that empowers every team member to navigate even the grayest of areas with confidence. Because you're united by clearly defined values and a principled decision-making process, you can thoughtfully weigh challenges from multiple angles. Personal ethics seamlessly align with corporate responsibility. Ethics become not a burden, but a paradigm for innovation that expands possibilities. The outcome is a culture of unshakable credibility and accountability. Whether it's your employees, customers, investors or the wider community - stakeholders know they can trust your moral fiber. You're an organization that prioritizes more than just profits, but standing for something bigger.

By institutionalizing ethics as a inviolable practice, you cement a foundation for enduring success defined by more than just revenues. You create a legacy of integrity that will continue inspiring principled leadership for generations to come. This is how truly great companies create positive ripple effects that transform industries and communities.

Balancing Stakeholder Interests:

Leaders must balance the often-conflicting interests of employees, investors, customers, and the community. This requires skill, a strong ethical foundation, and clear communication. For example, cost-cutting may satisfy shareholders but lead to layoffs, damaging morale and product quality. Navigating such challenges demands transparency about the rationale behind decisions and upholding principles of fairness and respect for all stakeholders.

In a truly ethical organization, leaders foster an environment where raising concerns is welcomed, not silenced. They actively cultivate diverse perspectives, knowing varying viewpoints strengthen collective ethical judgment. Employees feel empowered to voice ideas for upholding integrity, creating a culture of shared accountability. This open and inclusive approach fortifies the organization's ethical foundation over time.

Ethical Dilemmas in Leadership:

Leaders often encounter situations that challenge their values and ethics. For instance, discovering that a profitable client is misusing your product in ways that violate company standards. The choice to maintain or end this relationship extends beyond business considerations; it reflects your leadership and the organization's principles. These decisions can have far-reaching consequences, impacting not only the company's reputation but also its employees, customers, and the broader community.

Handling such dilemmas with transparency and consistency reinforces a culture of ethical decision-making. By openly communicating the reasoning behind these difficult choices and ensuring they align with the company's moral compass, leaders demonstrate their commitment to integrity. Ultimately, fostering an environment where ethical behavior is the norm contributes to the long-term success and sustainability of the company.

The Role of Values in Ethical Leadership:

The values you hold and promote as a leader profoundly impact your organization's ethical climate. Clearly defined personal and organizational values act as a compass that guides decisions and actions across all levels of the company. These values should be communicated frequently and integrated into the company's policies, training programs, and performance evaluation systems. For example, if integrity is a core value, this should be reflected not just in compliance policies but also in daily business operations and in how you deal with partners, suppliers, and competitors.

Ethical Decision-Making Exercise:

To further integrate the concept of ethical decision-making in your leadership practice, consider the following exercise designed to enhance your ethical reasoning.

Scenario:

Imagine your company has the opportunity to enter a lucrative deal that will significantly increase your market share but involves partnering with another company known for environmental violations.

Reflective Questions:

1. What are the potential ethical issues in this scenario?
2. How does this situation align with your core values and those of your company?
3. What are the short-term and long-term consequences of entering this deal?
4. What would be the most ethical action to take, and why?

This exercise encourages you to apply the ethical frameworks discussed and explore the complexities of real-world business decisions, enhancing your ability to lead with integrity and foresight. By embedding strong ethical principles into your leadership style, you aren't only foraging a path of integrity but also inspire those around you to commit to a higher standard of conduct. A culture of trust and respect, which are indispensable assets in today's business environment. Remember that each decision you make contributes to the legacy of your leadership and the enduring success of your organization.

7.2 Building and Maintaining Trust through Transparency

Hamdi Ulukaya, the founder and CEO of Chobani, is a great example of a leader who has built and maintained trust through transparency. When Ulukaya founded Chobani in 2005, he was committed to creating a company that was built on the principles of transparency, integrity, and social responsibility.

One way that Ulukaya has demonstrated transparency is by being open and honest about Chobani's business practices and supply chain. He has made it a priority to source high-quality, natural ingredients from local farmers and to be transparent about where Chobani's products come from. Ulukaya has also been transparent about Chobani's social and environmental impact. He has made it a priority to give back to the communities where Chobani operates, through initiatives like the Chobani Foundation, which supports entrepreneurship and economic development in underserved areas.

In addition, Ulukaya has been transparent about his own background and experiences as a Kurdish immigrant to the United States. He has used his platform as a business leader to advocate for refugees and immigrants, and to promote diversity and inclusion in the workplace. He has built a strong foundation of trust with his employees, customers, and stakeholders. His example demonstrates the importance of transparency in leadership, and how it can help to build and maintain trust over the long term.

Ulukaya's commitment to transparency has not only helped to build trust in Chobani, but has also inspired other business leaders to prioritize transparency and social responsibility in their own organizations. His leadership serves as a model for how transparency can be a powerful tool for building and maintaining trust in business and beyond.

A Foundation for Trust:

The product recall scenario is a great example of how transparency can make or break trust with customers and stakeholders. Companies that try to hide issues, shift blame, or downplay the seriousness of the situation often face a severe erosion of trust that can be difficult to recover from. On the flip side, those that are upfront about the problem, take ownership, clearly communicate the steps they are taking to rectify it, and show genuine concern for customer wellbeing can often weather the storm and even emerge with their reputation intact.

Of course, implementing a culture of transparency is easier said than done, especially for organizations that have operated differently in the past. It requires commitment from leadership to model the right behaviors, as well as investment in the systems, processes and training to support open communication. There may be short-term pains as previously hidden issues come to light. But the long-term gains in trust, engagement, and performance are well worth it.

As business leaders, we have a responsibility to build organizations that are resilient, innovative and trusted. Committing to transparency in all aspects of operations is a crucial step in that direction. When we are open and honest - in good times and bad - we show respect for our employees, customers and communities. We build trust through our actions.

Practical Transparency Practices:

Using transparency in leadership doesn't mean sharing trade secrets or making all internal discussions public. It's about carefully thinking about what to share, how to share it, and when. For example, when making decisions that impact your team or stakeholders, include them in the process as much as you can. This could mean having regular strategy meetings where team members can share their thoughts and feel truly involved in the company's direction. Keeping communication channels open is key. Tools like internal newsletters, regular town hall meetings, and open-door policies help create a two-way conversation that keeps everyone informed and engaged. That is the foundation of enduring success.

Digital platforms can provide real-time updates on project statuses, company news, and strategic changes, ensuring that all team members have access to the same information at the same time. This avoids any miscommunication or feelings of exclusion that might arise from delayed or inconsistent messaging. These platforms can serve as forums for feedback and discussion, allowing employees to ask questions, express concerns, and provide suggestions, which can lead to improvements in processes and policies.

The Impact of Transparency on Trust:

The correlation between transparency and trust is well-documented. Studies have shown that organizations that practice transparency not only enjoy higher levels of trust among their employees but also perform better in terms of customer loyalty and financial performance. In fact, transparent companies often achieve greater market valuations and attract more investments, as stakeholders perceive them as less risky compared to their more opaque counterparts.

This transparency extends beyond financial disclosures; it also encompasses the sharing of challenges and failures. When leaders are honest about setbacks and proactive in communicating corrective actions, it reassures employees and stakeholders that the organization is committed to learning and growth, rather than concealment and status quo.

Consider a scenario where a company faces unexpected financial difficulties. By proactively sharing this information with employees and explaining the steps being taken to mitigate the situation, the company can maintain staff morale and commitment. This open approach helps prevent the rumor mill from creating unnecessary anxiety and ensures that the workforce is part of the solution, rather than feeling victimized by the circumstances

Rebuilding Trust through Transparency:

Restoring trust after it has been broken is one of the hardest things a leader might have to do, but transparency is essential in this sensitive process. Begin by openly admitting the problem and taking full responsibility without blaming others. This shows accountability and maturity, setting the stage for rebuilding trust. Then, explain what is being done to fix the situation and stop it from happening again. This might involve changing policies, adding new checks and balances, or even changing leadership structures.

For example, after a data breach, a company should quickly inform affected parties and take clear steps to improve their cybersecurity measures. They should also provide regular updates about what is being done to secure data in the future. This type of transparent response can help restore customer confidence and repair the company's reputation. Think about using this chance to engage with stakeholders through surveys or feedback forms to understand their concerns and expectations going forward. This shows a commitment not just to internal improvement but also to the needs and opinions of those affected by your organization's actions. By including their feedback in your recovery plans, you rebuild trust on a foundation of inclusivity and responsiveness.

7.3 Integrity in Leadership: Actions Speak Louder than Words

John Mackey, the co-founder and CEO of Whole Foods Market, is a prime example of a leader who demonstrates integrity through his actions. Mackey has built Whole Foods on a foundation of values that prioritize healthy living, environmental sustainability, and ethical business practices.

Under Mackey's leadership, Whole Foods has established a reputation for providing high-quality, natural and organic products, and for being a socially responsible corporate citizen. Mackey has implemented a number of initiatives that demonstrate his commitment to integrity, including:

1. Establishing strict quality standards for the products sold in Whole Foods stores, and refusing to compromise on these standards even if it means higher costs or lower profits.
2. Implementing a salary cap for executives, which ensures that the highest-paid employee does not make more than 19 times the average worker's salary.
3. Donating 5% of Whole Foods' profits to charitable causes each year, and encouraging employees to volunteer in their communities.
4. Investing in renewable energy and other sustainable business practices, and setting ambitious goals for reducing Whole Foods' environmental footprint.

Mackey's actions have spoken louder than words, and have helped to build trust and loyalty among Whole Foods' customers, employees, and stakeholders. His leadership demonstrates that integrity is not just about what a leader says, but what they do, and how they embody their values in their actions and decisions.

Consistency Between Words and Actions:

Integrity is often touted as a core value, but it is the consistent alignment of words and actions that truly embeds this principle into the fabric of an organization. As a leader, your actions are constantly scrutinized, and any discrepancy between what you say and what you do can greatly undermine your credibility and authority.

Think about a situation where a leader says they support work-life balance but often sends emails late at night or on weekends. This behavior sends a confusing message to employees, suggesting that, despite what was said, the real expectation is to put work before personal time. To create a culture of integrity, it's essential that your actions not only match your words but also strengthen the values you want to promote within your team. This consistency between what you say and what you do serves as a powerful example for employees, showing that the principles you support are not just ideas but real commitments.

Keeping this consistency takes intentional effort, especially when making decisions where you must make sure that the choices reflect the values you encourage. For instance, if transparency and honesty are among your core values, then decision-making should involve open discussions and sharing of information instead of secret meetings or keeping information from others. By making these values part of everyday practices, you strengthen the foundation of integrity that trust and respect are built on. This alignment also gives employees a clear understanding of what is expected of them and how they should work, which can improve overall organizational unity and effectiveness.

Consequences of Compromising:

The consequences of compromising the integrity can be far-reaching, affecting not just immediate team morale but also broader organizational reputation. When leaders choose expediency over ethics, they risk creating a culture where shortcuts and ethical breaches become the norm rather than the exception. This erosion of ethical standards can lead to significant issues such as decreased employee loyalty, customer distrust, and ultimately, a tarnished brand reputation.

In the long run, the cost of repairing this damage far exceeds the temporary gains from unethical shortcuts. To illustrate, a company caught falsifying product quality reports might initially save on production costs. The eventual public disclosure of such actions can lead to massive recalls, legal penalties, and a lost customer base that can take years to rebuild, if at all.

Integrity Under Pressure:

These are precisely the moments when ethical leadership is most crucial. Strategies to uphold integrity in these situations include having a clear ethical protocol for decision-making that provides a guideline on how to act in various scenarios. Building a supportive network of advisors and confidants within and outside the organization can provide you with perspectives and advice that help maintain ethical clarity.

Frequently reviewing and thinking about your core values and the type of leader you want to be can also strengthen your commitment to integrity, serving as a moral guide during challenging times. Modeling integrity isn't just about avoiding bad actions, but actively showing ethical behavior. This active demonstration can take many forms, from how you handle private information and manage conflicts of interest, to how you treat each employee and conduct your business dealings.

Modeling Integrity:

An effective way to model integrity is to openly discuss the ethical challenges and how they were handled during team meetings or company-wide communications. For instance, sharing a case where you turned down a lucrative but ethically questionable project not only reinforces the organization's commitment to ethical practices, but also opens up discussions about ethics that can reinforce this culture across all levels of the organization. Another powerful method is to recognize and reward ethical behaviors exhibited by employees, which not only affirms those individuals but also sets a tangible example for others to follow.

Leaders are often closely watched for their ethical behavior. Staying true to your principles of integrity will not only guide your organization through challenges but also inspire those around you to raise their own standards. Your commitment to doing what is right, especially when faced with easier, less ethical choices, shapes not just your legacy as a leader but the ethical character of the entire organization.

7.4 The Impact of Ethical Leadership on Company Culture

Shaping the Culture:

The impact of ethical leadership goes far beyond implementing policies and making decisions; it is deeply connected to the organization's culture. As a leader, your actions and decisions don't just affect immediate business results but also set a powerful example that shapes the organization's cultural fabric. This development of ethical norms becomes the driving force behind every employee interaction, business transaction, and strategic decision, fundamentally defining the company's identity and reputation.

In shaping such a culture, leaders play a critical role not only in setting the right examples but also in creating and enforcing policies that encourage ethical behavior. This involves developing clear guidelines that outline acceptable behaviors and procedures for reporting unethical conduct without fear of retaliation.

An Ethical Environment:

Ethical leadership isn't just about policies and procedures - it's about fostering a culture of trust, openness and shared accountability at every level. Imagine an environment where raising ethical concerns isn't met with hushed tones, but with earnest listening and a united commitment to upholding integrity.

To build this foundation, leaders empower their people through actions like implementing anonymous reporting channels, removing fear around speaking up. Ethics training becomes woven into regular development, equipping everyone with tools to navigate dilemmas. And the dialogue remains two-way through surveys and safe spaces for voicing concerns confidentially.

When you institutionalize ethics through this multi-faceted, human-centric approach, it permeates your culture authentically. Ethical decision-making becomes an ingrained reflex, a source of pride. And maintaining the highest standards transitions from a top down mandate to an energizing collaborative effort at every rung - driven by a palpable sense that doing the right thing isn't just expected, but wholeheartedly embodied.

Ethical Leadership and Employee Satisfaction:

Studies have consistently shown that when employees feel they are working in an environment of mutual trust and respect, where fair treatment is not just promised but actually practiced, their job satisfaction levels increase significantly. Ethical leadership tends to reduce conflicts and promote a cooperative work environment, further improving employee satisfaction and retention. Companies which ranked highly for ethical leadership practices also have lower turnover rates and higher employee engagement scores, highlighting the direct benefits of ethical leadership on employee morale and loyalty.

Ethical leadership also provides a significant competitive advantage in attracting top talent and customers. In today's socially aware market, both potential employees and consumers are increasingly making decisions based on the ethical reputation of companies. They are more likely to engage with a brand or an employer they see as responsible and ethical.

In today's increasingly complex world, upholding honesty and integrity can often feel like an uphill battle. We're constantly bombarded with pressures to compromise our values – whether it's the allure of cutting corners for personal gain, or rationalizing ethical lapses as "just how business gets done."

Yet, it's in these very moments when staying true to our moral compass matters most. Each choice to embrace authenticity over deception, no matter how small, is a pebble that creates ripples of positive change. It's how we inspire trust, model accountability, and ultimately cultivate the ethical foundations that allow communities and organizations to thrive sustainably.

Honesty may not always be the easiest path, but it's the one that fortifies our integrity over time. It's a constant journey of reaffirming our commitment to living with purpose and character, even when faced with temptation or adversity. For it is only through unwavering honesty that we can build the just, principled world we wish to see.

7.5 Leading by Example: Ethical Practices in Daily Operations

Kenneth Frazier, the former CEO of Merck & Co., is an excellent example of a leader who consistently demonstrated ethical practices in daily operations. During his tenure from 2011 to 2021, Frazier prioritized ethics, transparency, and social responsibility in the pharmaceutical giant's practices.

Under Frazier's leadership, Merck became the first pharmaceutical company to publicly report the average annual list and net price increases for its drugs, a move praised as a step towards greater transparency in an industry often criticized opaque pricing practices. Frazier also prioritized diversity and inclusion, implementing initiatives to increase the representation and establish mentorship and sponsorship programs for underrepresented groups.

Frazier was known for taking principled stances on social and political issues, such as his resignation from Donald Trump's American Manufacturing Council in protest of the president's response to the Charlottesville rally in 2017. He consistently prioritized ethics and social responsibility in Merck's daily operations, ensuring that business practices were transparent, fair, and aligned with the company's values through initiatives like the "Standards of Business Conduct."

Daily Decisions:

Ethical leadership is not just about making big decisions. It's also about the small, daily choices that together shape the ethical reputation of your company. For example, think about the routine approval of supplier contracts—a leader committed to ethical operations will make sure these contracts are not only profitable but also come from suppliers who follow fair labor practices and environmental standards. This commitment to ethical sourcing reflects a broader commitment to corporate social responsibility, strengthening a culture of integrity and ethical awareness at all levels of the organization.

Crisis Situations:

Imagine being backed into a corner, pressured to compromise your values for a business deal. Perhaps it's fudging numbers, withholding key information, or turning a blind eye to unethical practices. In that moment, the promise of profits or pleasing stakeholders can make dishonesty feel like the path of least resistance.

But deep down, you know that path is unsustainable - for your business and your peace of mind. Because once you cross that line into deception, it only gets easier to keep rationalizing future lapses. Bit by bit, your integrity erodes until you may no longer recognize the ethical foundation you once stood upon.

This is a pivotal crossroad where you must have the courage of your convictions. To look beyond the short-term transactional gains and ask yourself - at what cost to my authenticity? To the hard-earned trust and credibility, I've built over years of principled choices?

It's a moment to pause and remember why living and leading with unwavering honesty matters so profoundly. How it shapes not just your personal legacy, but the enduring culture of your organization. A legacy where ethics reign as the ultimate differentiator and marker of true success.

While saying no to that unethical deal may bring challenges, it's an integrity tax worth paying. Because it's only through uncompromising honesty that you preserve the ability to meet your own eyes in the mirror as a professional of strong moral fiber. And that self respect is a salve during even the toughest of tests.

Handling these crises ethically involves clear, compassionate, and open communication. It requires leaders to provide regular updates about the steps being taken to resolve the crisis and to be available to answer questions and address concerns. This level of openness helps to alleviate fears and build a united front, where both employees and customers feel they are part of the solution rather than passive bystanders.

Training and Development:

Consistent training and development in ethical practices are crucial for ensuring that ethical behavior is understood, valued, and integrated into the company culture. This training should not only focus on compliance with laws and regulations but also on real-life ethical dilemmas that employees might face in their specific roles. For example, sales teams could benefit from scenarios that explore the boundaries of ethical selling techniques, helping them understand where persuasive selling crosses into manipulation.

Regular workshops, e-learning modules, and even role-playing exercises can make these training sessions engaging and practical, giving employees the skills they need to act ethically in their work. Leadership development programs should have a strong focus on ethical decision-making, preparing future leaders to uphold and spread the organization's ethical standards. These programs could be enhanced with mentoring by senior leaders who exemplify strong ethical principles, providing emerging leaders with role models and guidance on navigating the ethical complexities of leadership roles.

Monitoring and Enforcing Ethical Standards:

Imagine an organization where ethical standards aren't just words on a plaque, but living, breathing values that permeate every decision and action. This ideal becomes reality when ethics move beyond policy into practice - when there are robust safeguards to ensure principles don't just gather dust.

At the core lies a culture of radical transparency and accountability. One where comprehensive audits, both internal and external, aren't treated as corporate annoyances but celebrated opportunities to validate integrity across all levels and operations. There's an authentic embrace that these checkpoints are what allow ethical commitments to be more than just lip service.

But true ethical backbone is also empowering every employee, no matter their standing, to be an active upstander without fear. By implementing rigorous anonymous reporting systems, you eliminate the disempowering silence that often allows misconduct to proliferate unchecked. Instead, you cultivate a psychologically safe environment where people know their ethical concerns will be taken with the utmost seriousness and promptly investigated.

For instance, a technology firm might use software to monitor compliance with data protection laws, automatically flagging potential breaches for further investigation. Similarly, a manufacturing company could conduct regular safety audits to ensure adherence to ethical labor practices, with findings reported directly to the board to underscore the importance of ethical compliance.

As you navigate the complexities of daily operations and crisis situations, remember that your commitment to ethical practices in these moments not only defines your leadership but also shapes the ethical landscape of your entire organization. By integrating ethics into every decision, actively training and developing your teams, and rigorously monitoring and enforcing standards, you create an organizational culture that is not only compliant but also morally robust.

"Management consists of controlling a group or a set of entities to accomplish a goal. Leadership refers to an individual's ability to influence, motivate, and enable others to contribute toward organizational success. Influence and inspiration separate leaders from managers, not power and control. Employees first, customers second."

- Vineet Nayar, former CEO of HCL Technologies, a global IT services company

Chapter 8
Communicating Effectively as a Leader

Picture walking into that conference room - a vibrant mix of fresh-faced millennials bubbling with audacious ideas and sage veterans who've seen it all before. As a leader, it's your role to masterfully connect with every individual in an authentic way that makes them feel truly heard and valued.

It means fluidly adapting your communication style - bringing high energy one moment to match the youth's spirited engagement, then shifting to provide grounding wisdom that resonates with seasoned experience. This intentional emotional attunement is what forges an inclusive environment where diverse perspectives harmonize into unstoppable collaboration.

By flexing your approach, you unite your multigenerational team through the powerful bonds of open and effective communication.

8.1 Active Listening Skills for Effective Leadership

Mary Barra, the CEO of General Motors (GM), is an excellent example of a leader who has effectively used active listening skills to drive organizational change and success. When Barra took over as CEO in 2014, GM faced challenges including a massive recall crisis and a need to adapt to the changing market conditions and consumer preferences.

Barra has led GM through these challenges by actively listening to employees, customers, and other stakeholders. She visits GM factories and offices around the world, holds town hall meetings with employees, and seeks out feedback and input from a wide range of sources. Through this process, Barra has gained valuable insights into the company's operations, culture, and opportunities for improvement.

Based on these insights, Barra has implemented changes at GM, such as streamlining decision-making processes, increasing investment in electric and autonomous vehicles, and focusing on customer-centric innovation. She has also emphasized building a more inclusive and diverse workforce, recognizing the importance of diversity of thought and perspective of innovation and success. By seeking out diverse perspectives, asking questions, and truly listening to the answers, leaders can gain valuable insights and develop strategies grounded in their organizations' realities.

Fundamentals of Active Listening:

At the core of effective communication lies the skill of active listening, which involves fully concentrating, understanding, responding, and then remembering what is being said. Unlike passive listening, where the listener may hear the words but not fully engage with them, active listening means fully immersing yourself in the conversation. It's about hearing the unsaid—understanding the underlying emotions and intentions behind the words.

Active listening helps you understand your team members' perspectives and concerns on a deeper level. It shows you value their input and want to support them. For example, if someone is worried about a deadline, active listening helps you appreciate not just the practical challenges, but also the stress they're under. This allows you to find solutions that are both effective and empathetic. Active listening builds trust, understanding and a supportive team environment.

Improving Emotional Intelligence Through Listening:

Active listening also plays a crucial role in enhancing your emotional intelligence as a leader. By attentively listening to your team members, you gain insights into their emotional states, which can be crucial for maintaining team morale and motivation. Emotional intelligence involves recognizing your own emotions and those of others, and managing these emotions to achieve better outcomes.

Active listening helps you pick up on subtle cues in someone's tone, pacing, and word choice that reveal their emotional state. If a normally cheerful team member seems hesitant or less enthusiastic, it may signal low morale or a personal problem. By noticing these signs early, you can have a timely conversation to address any issues before they affect the team's work. Responding to emotions with empathy strengthens relationships and builds trust and openness with your team.

Active Listening Techniques:

First, maintain eye contact. This non-verbal cue signals attentiveness and engagement. However, be mindful of cultural differences as direct eye contact may not be appropriate in all cultures. Next, use body language to show involvement—nod occasionally, lean forward slightly, and avoid crossing your arms, as these gestures convey your interest and openness to the conversation. Jot down their new ideas so the member feels validated.

Reflective responding involves paraphrasing or summarizing what the speaker has said to confirm your understanding. For example, you might say, "It sounds like you're feeling overwhelmed with the current project timeline, is that correct?" This not only demonstrates that you are listening but also clarifies any misunderstandings immediately. Avoid interrupting or finishing the speaker's sentences. Allow them the space to express their thoughts fully before you respond. This respect for their input encourages more open and honest communication.

Overcoming Barriers:

Despite its importance, active listening can be hindered by several barriers. External distractions, such as noise or phone notifications, can interrupt the flow of communication. Minimize these as much as possible during conversations, perhaps by holding discussions in a quiet room and silencing electronic devices.

Internal barriers, such as preconceived notions or biases, can also impede effective listening. You might subconsciously tune out information that contradicts your views or expectations. To overcome this, approach each conversation with an open mind, consciously setting aside your judgments and focusing solely on understanding the speaker's perspective.

Multitasking during conversations can significantly detract from your ability to listen actively. It's tempting to check emails or think about other tasks during discussions, but this split focus can cause you to miss key information and signals, reducing the effectiveness of your communication. Prioritize the conversation at hand, giving it your full attention. This not only improves your listening skills but also sets a respectful and professional tone for your interactions.

Mastering active listening makes you a more effective leader and creates a respectful, understanding team culture. It allows you to:

- Connect deeply with team members
- Grasp their needs and worries
- Navigate complex, diverse workplaces

Each conversation is a chance to strengthen relationships, gain insights, and lead your team to success. Keep practicing active listening to become a better leader.

8.2 Adapting Communication Styles to Your Audience

Tony Hsieh, the former CEO of Zappos, is an excellent example of a leader who successfully adapted his communication style to his audience. Known for his unconventional leadership approach, Hsieh focused on creating a strong company culture that prioritized happiness, service, and personal growth.

With employees, Hsieh emphasized transparency, autonomy, and self-management, encouraging them to take ownership of their work and make decisions based on their own judgment. When communicating with customers, Hsieh prioritized creating a personalized and memorable experience. He trained employees to go above and beyond in their interactions and encouraged them to build genuine relationships based on trust and rapport. Hsieh personally responded to customer inquiries and feedback, and engaged with them informally through social media.

When communicating with media and external stakeholders, Hsieh shared Zappos' unique story and culture authentically and engagingly, often using humor, storytelling, and personal anecdotes. By adapting his communication style to his audience, Hsieh built a strong and loyal following for Zappos.

Adapting Your Communication Style

Adapting your communication style to each individual is key to effective leadership. People process information in different ways, and understanding these differences can greatly improve how your message is received and understood. The four main communication styles are:

1. **Analytical:** Data-driven, logical, and detail-oriented
2. **Intuitive:** Big-picture thinkers who prefer concepts and ideas
3. **Functional:** Focused on processes, timelines, and action plans
4. **Personal:** Emphasis on emotional connection and relationships

By identifying and tailoring your approach to each style, you can communicate more effectively with diverse team members.

Analytical communicators prefer hard data, facts, and statistics. Intuitive communicators look for the big picture and avoid getting bogged down in details. They prefer hard data, facts, and statistics. Functional communicators need step-by-step details and thrive on process and comprehensive timelines. Personal communicators value emotional language and connection, focusing on the feelings and relationships between people involved.

Suppose you're presenting a new company strategy aimed at increasing market share. To an analytical communicator, you might highlight statistical growth projections and market analysis. For intuitive communicators, a broad overview of the strategic vision without excessive detail will resonate more. Functional communicators will appreciate a detailed plan of the strategy's implementation, and personal communicators will be motivated by discussions on how the strategy improves team dynamics or customer satisfaction

Tailoring Messages:

Lastly, perfecting the art of tailoring your communication to different stakeholders — employees, customers, partners, and investors — is key to your success as a leader. Each group has different expectations and needs that require specific messaging. For employees, communication that is motivational, clear about expectations, and open to feedback can enhance engagement and productivity.

When communicating with customers, understanding their needs and feedback about your products or services is crucial, and your messages should reflect that you value their input and are responsive to their needs. For business partners, maintaining open lines of communication, trust, and mutual respect are vital, requiring you to be clear, professional, and consistent. Investors, on the other hand, look for transparency and consistency in your communication, with a focus on strategic information and growth outcomes.

For example, when releasing a new product, your communication to customers might focus on the benefits and value of the product, accompanied by engaging visuals and a clear call to action. For employees, the focus might be on how this product fits into the broader company goals and their specific roles in its success. Partners might require detailed production and distribution plans, whereas investors will be interested in the expected impact on market share and return on investment.

Across Generations:

Encouraging team members to share personal stories and experiences can boost empathy and understanding across the organization. This can be done through casual "get to know you" sessions or structured team-building activities focused on personal sharing and connection. Such interactions break down barriers between team members and enrich understanding of diverse backgrounds and views, creating a more inclusive and supportive work environment.

Every empathetic interaction strengthens the social fabric of your organization. It builds a more connected, resilient team ready to face challenges together. Keep leading with empathy to weave a strong, unified team. Each personal connection is an investment in the social fabric of your organization, resulting in a team that is more connected, understanding, and equipped to handle any challenge with unity and resilience.

8.3 Navigating Difficult Conversations with Grace and Authority

Brené Brown, a renowned researcher, author, and speaker, is an excellent example of a leader who navigates difficult conversations with grace and authority. Known for her work on vulnerability, courage, and empathy, Brown tackles sensitive topics such as shame, fear, and resilience in her writings, talks, and interviews.

Brown's key strength is creating a safe and non-judgmental space for difficult conversations. She models vulnerability and authenticity by sharing her own struggles and experiences, inviting others to do the same. Brown emphasizes empathy and active listening, encouraging people to understand others' perspectives before rushing to judgment or offering advice.

At the same time, Brown speaks hard truths and challenges people to confront their biases and limitations with compassion and firmness, using research and storytelling to illustrate her points compellingly and accessibly.

In her book "Dare to Lead," Brown discusses the importance of having tough conversations about race, gender, and power in the workplace. She acknowledges the discomfort and fear that often accompany these conversations but argues that they are essential for creating truly inclusive and equitable organizations. Brown provides practical tools and frameworks for navigating these conversations with courage and skill, emphasizing self-awareness, curiosity, and a willingness to learn and grow.

Navigating difficult conversations is an integral skill for any leader, bearing significant impact on the well-being of both the team and the organization. These conversations, whether they involve addressing performance issues, discussing sensitive topics, or delivering unfavorable news, require a delicate balance of assertiveness and empathy. By preparing meticulously for these discussions, you can ensure that they are not only conducted smoothly but also lead to productive outcomes.

Preparation:

Effective communication, especially in high-stakes situations, relies heavily on preparation. Begin by clearly defining the purpose of the conversation, whether it's solving a problem, providing feedback, or discussing a sensitive topic. Clarifying this goal helps keep the discussion focused and ensures everyone is on the same page from the start.

Anticipate potential reactions from your team member by considering their perspective and preparing for various responses, such as defensiveness, upset, or agreement. This allows you to adapt your approach to their emotional and informational needs, making the conversation more productive and constructive.

Your preparation should also involve selecting an appropriate setting for the conversation. Opt for a private, neutral location that ensures confidentiality and minimizes distractions. This creates an environment conducive to open, honest communication without fear of judgment from others.

Come prepared with all relevant information, such as specific examples or data points that support your concerns or arguments. Being well-informed strengthens your position and demonstrates to your team member that you've approached the conversation with the seriousness and attention it warrants.

Maintaining Composure and Authority:

Maintaining composure and authority is crucial during these conversations, as it sets the tone for the interaction. Approach the discussion calmly, regardless of the topic's nature. Keeping your emotions in check creates a safe space for open dialogue and prevents the conversation devolving into an unproductive argument.

However, maintaining authority doesn't mean being inflexible or harsh. Instead, it involves asserting your position or the organization's policies firmly and clearly. Balancing this assertion with empathy helps address the issues at hand while preserving your team member's dignity and self-esteem.

Constructive Outcomes:

Using strategies that guide the conversation towards constructive outcomes is essential. One effective approach is using positive language that emphasizes solutions rather than dwelling on problems. For example, instead of saying, "You failed to meet the project deadline," you could say, "Let's explore how we can better manage timelines for future projects." This softens the criticism and encourages a forward-thinking mindset focused on improvement and growth.

Additionally, highlighting common goals and shared values helps align both parties and foster cooperation. By framing the conversation around mutual objectives and principles, you create a foundation for collaboration and problem-solving.

Reminding your team member that the ultimate objective is to enhance team performance and achieve organizational goals can motivate them to participate actively in finding solutions. Using inclusive language such as "we" and "us" instead of "you" can reinforce a sense of teamwork and shared responsibility.

Following Up After Difficult Conversations

Following up after difficult conversations is crucial to ensure that both parties clearly understand the outcomes and are committed to the agreed-upon actions. Schedule a follow-up meeting or send a summary email that outlines what was discussed, decisions made, and next steps. This keeps communication channels open and reinforces the importance of the issues addressed, ensuring they are dealt with appropriately.

Follow-up also allows you to offer additional support or resources to help your team member improve or adjust. This demonstrates your commitment to their development and success. By consistently following up after challenging conversations, you foster a culture of accountability, growth, and open communication within your team.

As you continue to engage in these critical discussions, keep in mind that your role as a leader is to guide your team towards growth and success. By approaching difficult conversations with empathy, clarity, and a solutions-oriented mindset, you create an environment where your team members feel heard, supported, and motivated to improve. Your commitment to effective communication during challenging times will undoubtedly contribute to the long-term success and cohesion of your team.

8.4 Utilizing Technology for Clear and Consistent Communication

Choosing the correct technology plays a vital role in facilitating communication in today's fast-paced business world. There are many tools available, from simple email to complex project management platforms. Choosing the right technology for your team's needs can greatly improve communication efficiency and clarity. When selecting tools, consider your team's size, the nature of your projects, and the level of interaction needed. Assessing these factors will help you find the best tools to support your team's communication, productivity, and collaboration.

Digital:

Digital communication platforms offer speed and efficiency that traditional methods can't match. Many digital tools also allow you to archive and search past communications, which is invaluable for tracking projects, maintaining continuity, and resolving disputes about who said what and when.

Digital Challenges:

Another significant challenge is the overwhelming volume of communication that digital tools can generate. This can lead to information overload where important messages are lost in a sea of notifications, reducing the overall effectiveness of communication. Encourage clarity and conciseness in all written communications. This involves using simple, direct language and structuring messages in a way that the main points are easy to discern. Using bullet points to break down complex information can help in highlighting key elements and ensuring that the message is not lost in unnecessary details.

Best Practices:

For sensitive or nuanced discussions, encourage face-to-face or phone conversations instead of written messages. This can help in conveying tone more effectively and allows for immediate clarification of any misunderstandings. Establish clear guidelines on the appropriate use of different communication platforms. For example, instant messaging may be reserved for urgent queries or casual interactions, while emails might be used for formal communications or when detailed records are necessary. Regular training sessions on effective digital communication can also help in ensuring that all team members are proficient in using the chosen platforms and are aware of the communication protocols, especially for those who have not grown up with technology.

It also involves being mindful of response times, maintaining confidentiality where required, and being respectful and courteous in all exchanges. It is evident that while digital tools offer significant advantages in terms of speed and efficiency, they also require careful management to avoid pitfalls like miscommunication and information overload. By choosing the right tools, adhering to best practices, and fostering professionalism, you can harness the full potential of digital communication to enhance connectivity and efficiency within your team.

"Just as managers have subordinates and leaders have followers, managers create circles of power while leaders create circles of influence."

— Vineet Nayar, Indian business executive and author

Chapter 9
Leadership in Strategic Planning and Execution

Picture yourself at the helm of a ship, navigating through misty waters with the duty of keeping everyone on board headed in the right direction. As a leader, you are not only steering the ship but also making sure that every member of your crew understands and aligns with the course you've set to reach your organization's objectives. This chapter delves into how you can synchronize team efforts with overarching organizational goals, a fundamental prerequisite for achieving sustainable success.

9.1 Aligning Team Efforts with Organizational Goals

Arne Sorenson, the former CEO of Marriott International, was a leader who successfully aligned team efforts with organizational goals. Known for his inclusive leadership style, Sorenson united his team around a shared vision of hospitality and service.

Sorenson emphasized Marriott's five core values - put people first, pursue excellence, embrace change, act with integrity, and serve our world - consistently communicating and modeling these values to ensure they were deeply ingrained in the company's culture and decision-making processes.

To align team efforts, Sorenson prioritized clear communication and transparency. He held regular town hall meetings with employees to share updates on the company's performance, strategy, and priorities, encouraging open dialogue and feedback to create a culture of trust and collaboration.

Sorenson also focused on employee development and empowerment, investing in training and leadership development programs to help employees build the skills and capabilities needed to succeed. He encouraged a culture of innovation and experimentation, giving teams autonomy and resources to pursue new ideas.

Finally, Sorenson's commitment to social responsibility and community engagement aligned the company's efforts with broader social and environmental goals, creating a sense of purpose that inspired team members to work together towards a common good.

Clarifying Organizational Vision and Goals:

A clear, communicable vision is the compass that guides your ship; it articulates where your organization is headed and why. It is imperative, therefore, that this vision is not only well-defined but also resonates with every member of your team. Think of your organizational vision as a story that every employee can say with conviction, one that they are a part of. This narrative should be compelling enough to motivate and drive the collective energy of your workforce towards achieving specific, measurable goals. For instance, a tech company might envision becoming the leader in sustainable technology by 2025, a goal that is both inspiring and quantifiable.

To ensure that this vision is effectively communicated, employ multiple channels and ensure consistency in your messaging. Regular meetings, newsletters, and interactive sessions where employees can ask questions and provide feedback play a crucial role in this process. It's also beneficial to visually display your vision and goals in common areas within the workplace to continually remind and inspire your team about the organization's aspirations.

Strategies for Effective Alignment:

Aligning individual efforts with organizational goals requires a strategic approach where every role is defined in terms of its contribution to the big picture. This alignment begins with meticulous job design and clear role descriptions that explicitly connect each position's responsibilities with overall organizational objectives. For example, if customer satisfaction is a key goal, then roles in customer service should have clearly defined metrics related to customer feedback scores and resolution times.

Training and development also play a crucial role in the alignment. Tailored training programs that not only focus on skill enhancement but also on how these skills directly relate to organizational goals can enhance role clarity and engagement. Furthermore, involving employees in the goal-setting process can significantly increase their commitment and understanding of organizational objectives. This participative approach makes the goals more personal and relevant, fostering a deeper commitment to achieving them.

Overcoming Alignment Challenges: One common issue is resistance from team members who may feel disconnected from organizational objectives or fear that new goals might disrupt their routines. Overcoming this resistance involves active listening, empathy, and inclusive leadership practices. It's crucial to address concerns openly and provide clear, logical explanations of how aligning with the broader goals benefits everyone—not just the organization but also individuals' professional growth.

Another challenge is the silo mentality, where departments or teams operate in isolation without regard for how their actions affect other parts of the organization. To combat this, foster an environment of collaboration and cross-departmental communication. Regular inter-departmental meetings and team-building activities can bridge gaps between different areas of your organization, ensuring a more unified and cohesive effort towards common goals.

Successful Alignment:

To illustrate successful alignment, consider the case of a multinational consumer goods company that realigned its teams to focus on digital innovation as a response to increasing e-commerce demand. The company clearly communicated its revised goals through a series of workshops and interactive Q&A sessions, helping employees understand their role in this new strategy. Departments worked collaboratively on projects such as improving online customer interfaces and optimizing digital marketing strategies. The result was a significant increase in online sales and improved customer satisfaction rates, proving the effectiveness of strategic alignment in organizational success.

In another example, a non-profit organization focused on environmental conservation aligned its team efforts by embedding its mission into every role. From administrative staff to field workers, every employee was encouraged to contribute ideas on how to better conserve resources and promote sustainability within their scope of work. This inclusive approach not only enhanced role clarity and employee engagement but also led to innovative projects that significantly advanced the organization's mission.

These examples underscore the transformative power of aligning team efforts with organizational goals. As you continue to navigate the complex waters of business leadership, remember that a clear vision, strategic alignment, empathetic leadership, and proactive communication are your best tools for ensuring that every member of your team is rowing in the same direction.

9.2 Strategic Decision-Making: Balancing Short-term Needs with Long-Term Vision

Allgood Provisions is a small artisanal food company that produces organic and locally sourced jams, jellies, and chutneys. Founded in 2010 with a focus on sustainability and ethical sourcing, the company has built a loyal following in the local community and has recently started expanding into regional markets.

In 2022, Allgood Provisions faced a pivotal decision. A major national retailer approached them with an opportunity to supply their products to stores across the country. While this would provide a significant short-term revenue boost, it would also require a substantial increase in production capacity and potentially compromise their commitment to sourcing locally.

After careful deliberation, the company's founders decided to pursue a mixed approach. They accepted the national retailers offer but limited their distribution to a smaller geographic region, allowing them to maintain their local sourcing practices while still benefiting from the increased revenue stream. Additionally, they invested a portion of the proceeds into expanding their production facilities and equipment, ensuring they could meet the increased demand while maintaining their commitment to quality and sustainability.

Strategic Decision Making:

When leading your organization through both calm and turbulent times, it's crucial to make strategic decisions that balance immediate needs with your company's long-term vision. Implementing scenario planning, which involves creating detailed, imagined scenarios to test the potential impacts of different decisions. This method allows you to visualize the possible outcomes of strategic choices and assess their long-term implications.

For example, if you're considering expanding into a new market, scenario planning can help you explore various market entry strategies and their potential impacts on your existing operations. By preparing for multiple scenarios, you can develop flexible strategies that allow you to quickly adapt to changing market conditions or internal business challenges while staying focused on your long-term goals.

The Role of Data in Strategic Decisions:

In today's digital age, data plays a crucial role in strategic decision-making. Data-driven decisions not only reduce uncertainty but also enhance the credibility of the choices made. By grounding your decisions in data, you're more likely to align your short-term actions with your long-term strategic goals.

For example, if your long-term goal is to improve customer satisfaction, analyzing customer feedback data can help you identify immediate improvements in customer service processes. Advanced analytics and business intelligence tools can provide deeper insights into trends and patterns that impact your business, helping you anticipate future challenges and opportunities. By leveraging data in your decision-making process, you can make more informed, objective, and strategic choices that drive your organization's success.

Establish clear guidelines on how data should be collected, analyzed, and interpreted to ensure consistency and reliability in your decision-making processes. This will help create a common understanding of data's role and value across the organization.

By building the necessary infrastructure and promoting a data-centric culture, you can harness the power of data to make informed, strategic decisions that drive your organization's long-term success while addressing immediate needs.

Navigating Trade-offs and Compromises:

Strategic decision-making often involves making difficult trade-offs and compromises, particularly when short-term operational needs conflict with long-term strategic goals. Effective leaders understand that some trade-offs, while challenging, are necessary to achieve the best possible outcomes for the organization. The key is to comprehend the implications of these trade-offs and manage them proactively.

For example, deciding to cut costs in the short term by reducing research and development expenditure might negatively impact long-term innovation. In such cases, it's crucial to weigh the immediate financial benefits against potential long-term strategic setbacks. Leaders must carefully consider the consequences of their decisions and strive to find a balance that optimizes both short-term and long-term outcomes.

By approaching trade-offs with a strategic mindset and a willingness to make tough decisions, leaders can navigate the complexities of balancing the immediate needs with long-term goals, ultimately steering their organizations towards sustained success.

One method to manage these trade-offs effectively is through cost-benefit analysis, which helps quantify the gains and losses associated with different decision options. This analysis can be complemented by risk assessment techniques that evaluate the potential risks associated with each trade-off. By understanding both the benefits and the risks, you can make more informed decisions that balance short-term needs with long-term objectives.

Developing a Strategic Mindset:

This involves thinking beyond day-to-day operations and focusing on the broader impact of decisions. It requires being visionary, anticipating future trends, and preparing the organization to meet upcoming challenges and seize opportunities.

Regular strategic review sessions can facilitate the development of this mindset. During these sessions, leaders reflect on the organization's strategic direction and make necessary adjustments. This practice encourages stepping back from immediate operational concerns and re-focusing on long-term goals.

By adopting a strategic mindset and regularly reviewing organizational strategy, leaders can make well-informed decisions that balance short-term needs with long-term objectives, ultimately guiding their organizations towards sustained success in an everchanging business landscape. Fostering this mindset within your organization involves encouraging your team to think strategically. This can be achieved by involving them in the strategic planning process and encouraging them to contribute their insights and ideas. Providing training and development opportunities that enhance their understanding of the business's strategic goals can also empower them to make decisions that align with these goals.

9.3 Leading Change: Strategies for Effective Implementation

Greenly, a boutique marketing agency with 35 employees, recognized the need to adapt to the rapidly evolving digital landscape. The company's leadership team decided to transition from traditional marketing methods to a more data-driven, digital-first approach.

To lead this change effectively, Greenly implemented several strategies:

1. **Clear communication:** The leadership team held company-wide meetings to explain the rationale behind the change, address concerns, and outline the benefits for both the company and employees.
2. **Employee involvement:** Greenly formed a cross-

functional team comprising representatives from various departments to provide input and feedback during the transition process.
3. **Training and development:** The company invested in comprehensive training programs to upskill employees in digital marketing techniques, data analysis, and relevant software tools.
4. **Pilot projects:** Before a full-scale implementation, Greenly ran pilot projects with select clients to test their new digital strategies, allowing for adjustments and refinements.
5. **Incentives and recognition:** Employees who embraced the change and demonstrated proficiency in the new skills were recognized and rewarded, encouraging further adoption.
6. **Continuous improvement:** Greenly established regular review sessions to assess progress, identify areas for improvement, and make necessary adjustments.

By combining clear communication, employee engagement, training, gradual implementation, and a culture of continuous improvement, Greenly successfully navigated the transition to a digital-first marketing approach, positioning the company for long-term growth and success in the evolving industry landscape.

Change Principles:

Stakeholder engagement begins by identifying all parties affected by the change and understanding their interests and concerns. It involves bringing them into the conversation and making them an active part of the change process. For example, if a company implements a new IT system, it will affect the tech team deploying it and the end-users interacting with it daily. Engaging stakeholders early helps understand their needs and address apprehensions through workshops, meetings, or informal conversations. These interactions gather valuable insights and make stakeholders feel valued and understood. By actively involving all parties, leaders can ensure a smoother transition and greater buy-in for the change initiative.

Clear communication is another pillar of effective change management. It involves articulating the reasons for the change, the benefits it aims to bring, and the steps that will be taken to implement it. This communication should be consistent, frequent, and through multiple channels to ensure that it reaches everyone in the organization. For example, email updates, intranet posts, and regular team meetings can be effective ways to keep everyone informed. The goal is to eliminate any ambiguity about the change, thereby reducing anxiety and resistance among employees.

Resistance To Change:

Addressing resistance is one of the most challenging aspects of managing change. Resistance can arise from fear of the unknown, discomfort with new procedures, or perceived threats to job security. Leaders must identify these resistance points early and address them with empathy.

One effective strategy is involving resistant team members in the change process. Giving them a role or voice in how the change is implemented can transform resistance into cooperation. Additionally, providing training and support helps ease the transition, making the change less daunting for employees. By proactively addressing resistance through involvement, empathy, and support, leaders can navigate the challenges of change management and foster a more adaptable, resilient organization.

Role of Leaders:

Leaders play a crucial role in driving and supporting change initiatives. They are not just decision-makers but also motivators and role models. Their attitude towards the change significantly influences how the rest of the organization reacts.

Leaders need to embody the change they want to see by being the first to adopt new processes, tools, or behaviors. This sets a visible example for others to follow. Moreover, leaders should be accessible and approachable, ready to listen to concerns and provide support where needed. By remaining positive, responsive, and proactive, leaders can drive the momentum of the change process, making the transition smoother and more successful. Their ability to lead by example and provide ongoing support is key to navigating the challenges of change management and fostering a culture of adaptability and resilience within the organization.

Evaluation:

Assessing the impact of change initiatives is essential for gauging their effectiveness and enabling continuous improvement. This evaluation should take into account both quantitative and qualitative metrics. For instance, if a new sales strategy was implemented, quantitative measures could include changes in sales figures, customer acquisition rates, and market share, while qualitative indicators might involve employee satisfaction and customer feedback on the new sales process. Utilizing tools such as surveys, performance data analysis, and customer feedback forms can be invaluable in collecting this information.

The evaluation process not only highlights successes and failures but also yields insights that can be leveraged to refine future change initiatives, ensuring that each successive effort is more effective than the last. By consistently evaluating the impact of change, leaders can make informed decisions, refine their strategies, and foster a culture of ongoing improvement within the organization.

When implementing these change management strategies, it's important to remember that the goal is not just to introduce new ways of doing things but to do so in a manner that is inclusive, well-communicated, and effectively integrated into the company's fabric. This thoughtful approach ensures that change is not merely implemented but embraced, leading to improved performance and a stronger, more adaptable organization.

As you move forward with your change initiatives, keep these principles in mind to guide your actions and decisions. By prioritizing inclusivity, clear communication, and effective integration, you can ensure that each step you take is a step towards a more dynamic and resilient future for your organization. Embrace change as an opportunity for growth and improvement, and lead your team with empathy, transparency, and a steadfast commitment to success.

9.4 Measuring Success: KPIs for Leadership and Team Performance

TechByte Solutions, a 60-person software firm, established the following KPIs to evaluate the effectiveness of their leadership and team performance:

1. **Project Delivery:** They tracked the percentage of projects delivered on time and within budget. This metric helped assess project management skills, resource allocation, and team collaboration.
2. **Customer Satisfaction:** TechByte actively sought feedback from clients through surveys and reviews, measuring customer satisfaction rates and addressing any concerns promptly.
3. **Employee Engagement:** Regular anonymous surveys gauged employee satisfaction, motivation, and commitment levels, providing insights into the leadership's ability to foster a positive work culture.
4. **Talent Retention:** By monitoring employee turnover rates and conducting exit interviews, TechByte aimed to identify and address any issues that could lead to talent loss.
5. **Revenue Growth:** While focusing on sustainable growth, TechByte tracked year-over-year revenue increases, indicating the effectiveness of their business strategies and leadership decisions.
6. **Innovation Metrics:** The company measured the number of new product features, patents, or process improvements generated, reflecting the team's creativity and ability to adapt to market changes.

Identifying Relevant KPIs:

By regularly reviewing and analyzing these KPIs, TechByte's leadership could identify areas for improvement, make data-driven decisions, and implement strategies to enhance overall leadership effectiveness and team performance.

In the realm of strategic leadership, the adage "what gets measured gets managed" rings particularly true. It highlights the critical role of Key Performance Indicators (KPIs) in not only tracking the effectiveness of your team's efforts but also in steering these efforts towards achieving your strategic goals. Identifying the right KPIs requires a deep understanding of your organization's objectives and a clear vision of what success looks like.

When implementing change management strategies, remember that the goal is not just to introduce new ways of doing things but to do so inclusively, with clear communication and effective integration into the company's fabric. This thoughtful approach ensures that change is not merely implemented but embraced, leading to improved performance and a stronger, more adaptable organization.

Prioritize inclusivity, clear communication, and effective integration to ensure each step takes you closer to a more dynamic and resilient future for your organization. Embrace change as an opportunity for growth and improvement, and lead your team with empathy, transparency, and a steadfast commitment to success.

Set Clear Targets:

Once these KPIs are identified, the next step is setting clear and achievable performance targets. These targets should be challenging yet realistic, motivating your team to excel but not so high that they become demoralizing. Effective communication plays a crucial role in this stage—every team member needs to understand not only what the targets are, but also why they are important. This understanding fosters a sense of ownership and commitment to achieving these goals.

Continuous Improvement:

If a particular KPI related to customer response times is consistently underperforming, this could trigger a review of your customer service processes. Perhaps additional training is needed for your customer service team, or maybe the current software is inadequate and needs upgrading. By regularly analyzing these KPIs, you can identify trends, anticipate issues before they become problems, and continuously refine your strategies to better meet your organizational goals.

Balancing Quantitative and Qualitative Measures

Balancing quantitative and qualitative measures are essential for a well-rounded view of performance. Quantitative KPIs, such as sales revenue or production costs, provide concrete, easily measurable data. On the other hand, qualitative measures, like team morale or customer satisfaction, offer insights that are not as easily quantified but are equally important.

For example, high team morale can significantly enhance productivity and reduce turnover, while high customer satisfaction can lead to increased loyalty and positive word-of-mouth, both of which are crucial for long-term success. Tools such as employee satisfaction surveys or customer feedback forms can be invaluable in gathering this qualitative data, providing a deeper understanding of the underlying factors affecting your KPIs.

By considering both quantitative and qualitative measures, you can gain a more comprehensive picture of your organization's performance and make informed decisions that drive success.

In incorporating these strategies, remember that the goal of using KPIs is not just to track where your team and organization stand but to foster an environment of ongoing improvement and strategic alignment.

9.5 Succession Planning: Preparing for Leadership Transitions

Luminous Tech, a boutique software development firm with 75 employees, recognized the importance of succession planning to ensure business continuity and smooth leadership transitions. The company's founders, who had built the business from the ground up, were approaching retirement age and wanted to secure the future of their organization.

Luminous Tech embarked on a comprehensive succession planning process, starting with identifying high-potential employees who demonstrated strong leadership qualities, technical expertise, and a deep understanding of the company's values and culture. These individuals were enrolled in leadership development programs, mentored by senior executives, and given opportunities to lead cross-functional projects.

Importance of a Plan:

The founders implemented a gradual transition plan, gradually delegating more responsibilities and decision-making authority to the identified successors. This hands-on approach allowed the successors to gain practical experience while still benefiting from the founders' guidance and support.

To further support the transition process, Luminous Tech established a formal knowledge transfer system, documenting essential processes, best practices, and institutional knowledge. This ensured that critical information was not lost during the leadership change.

Steps in Developing a Succession Plan:

Open communication and transparency were maintained throughout the succession planning process, keeping employees informed and engaged. This approach helped build trust and support for the incoming leadership while ensuring a seamless transition. By minimizing disruptions to the company's operations and client relationships, the organization demonstrated its commitment to stability and continuity.

Effective succession planning ensures that no key leadership position is left vacant or inadequately filled due to unforeseen circumstances. It involves identifying and nurturing potential leaders who can seamlessly take over senior roles when needed. For any organization that values resilience and aims for continuity in its strategic operations, having a succession plan is not an option—it's a necessity.

By prioritizing succession planning and maintaining open communication, organizations can navigate leadership transitions with confidence, ensuring a stable and successful future.

Developing a comprehensive succession plan starts with clearly understanding the organization's long-term goals and identifying the specific leadership roles critical for achieving these objectives. The next step is to identify potential successors for these key positions based on a combination of leadership competencies, experience, and potential for future growth, rather than solely on seniority or tenure.

To highlight employees with the necessary skills and attributes for effective leadership, organizations can utilize:

1. Performance appraisals
2. Leadership assessments
3. Feedback from direct reports and peers

These tools provide valuable insights into an individual's capabilities and potential, allowing the organization to make informed decisions when selecting candidates for succession planning.

After identifying potential leaders, the focus shifts to providing them with development opportunities to prepare for future roles. This can include targeted training, mentoring by current leaders, rotational assignments across different departments, and external education programs. Each of these opportunities should be designed to fill gaps in knowledge and experience and expose potential leaders to the challenges they would face in their new roles.

Ongoing feedback on their progress is crucial, allowing them to continually refine their skills. By investing in the development of high-potential employees, organizations can build a strong pipeline of future leaders who are well-prepared to take on senior roles when the need arises. This proactive approach to succession planning ensures a smooth transition and continuity of leadership, even in the face of unexpected changes.

Succession Challenges:

However, succession planning is often fraught with challenges. One of the most common issues is the resistance from current leaders, who may view the development of potential successors as a threat to their own position. To mitigate this, it's important to foster a culture that views succession planning as a positive and essential aspect of professional development for everyone in the organization.

Another significant challenge is ensuring the diversity of the leadership pipeline. Often, unconscious biases might influence the selection of candidates, leading to a succession pool that lacks diversity in thought, experience, and background. Organizations need to be deliberate in creating diversity and inclusion strategies that permeate their succession planning processes.

Advantages:

Succession planning offers more than just a safety net; it provides a strategic advantage. Organizations with a clear approach to succession are more likely to engage and retain high-performing employees, as these individuals see a clear path for career advancement. Moreover, by aligning the development of potential leaders with the strategic goals of the organization, companies ensure that their future leaders are not only equipped to handle the roles but are also fully aligned with the company's long-term vision and culture.

In this dynamic business environment, where change is the only constant, the ability to seamlessly transition leadership without disrupting the strategic momentum of the organization is invaluable. Succession planning, when executed effectively, serves as a critical lever for sustainable growth, enabling organizations to navigate the complexities of change with confidence and integrity. The goal is to build not just a pipeline of leaders, but a legacy of visionary guidance that will steer the organization towards continued success.

"Leadership is unlocking people's potential to become better."

- Bill Bradley, American politician and former professional basketball player, serving as a U.S. Senator from New Jersey from 1979 to 1997.

Chapter 10
Cultivating Leadership at Every Level

Think of your team like a diverse garden, with each person at a different stage of growth. As a leader, you must recognize and nurture the unique leadership potential in every team member. This means identifying which individuals need more support, which ones are ready for new challenges, and which ones are primed for leadership roles. By cultivating leadership at every level of your organization, you create a sustainable and thriving environment that benefits both individual careers and the overall success of your business.

10.1 Identifying and Nurturing Potential Leaders Within Your Team

BDO Digital Solutions is a multimillion-dollar company which provides strategic technology and business advisory services. They also have a special partnership with the Alain Locke Charter School to promote technology-driven initiatives including a robotics club and coding and programming club. BDO has implemented the following strategies to identify and nurture potential leaders within their company.

1. **Performance evaluations:** Employees are regularly evaluated not just for their technical skills and project delivery but also on leadership qualities such as strategic thinking, decision-making abilities, communication skills, and team management.
2. **360-degree feedback:** Feedback is gathered from an employee's peers, direct reports (if applicable), and managers to gain a well-rounded perspective on their leadership potential and areas for development.
3. **Talent review sessions:** Companies hold regular talent review meetings where high potential employees are discussed, and development plans are created for those identified as future leaders.
4. **Mentorship programs:** High-potential employees are paired with more experienced leaders who serve as mentors, providing guidance, coaching, and sharing their leadership experiences.
5. **Leadership training:** Potential leaders are provided with specialized training programs, workshops, and coaching focused on developing critical leadership

competencies such as strategic thinking, change management, emotional intelligence, and executive presence.
6. **Stretch assignments:** Employees are given challenging assignments or projects that stretch their abilities and expose them to new responsibilities, preparing them for future leadership roles.
7. **Executive sponsorship:** Senior leaders take an active role in sponsoring and advocating for high-potential employees, providing them with visibility and opportunities for growth.

BDO Digital uses these strategies to identify and nurture their future leaders from within their existing talent pool.

Spotting Leadership Potential:

Identifying potential leaders within your team is like a miner sifting through rocks to find gems—it requires patience, insight, and a keen eye for the unpolished signs of leadership qualities. Potential leaders often demonstrate a combination of strong communication skills, decisiveness, and the ability to inspire and motivate others.

However, they also exhibit less obvious traits such as resilience in the face of challenges, a propensity for strategic thinking, and the capacity for empathy. These individuals often go above and beyond their job descriptions, show a deep commitment to the organization's values, and proactively seek solutions to problems. By recognizing and nurturing these qualities, you can uncover the hidden leadership potential within your team and help these individuals grow into effective leaders.

To identify potential leaders, create an environment that allows leadership traits to be demonstrated. Encourage open communication, collaborative projects, and problem solving initiatives where individuals can showcase their capabilities and leadership qualities. Regular performance reviews can evaluate not only their current role performance but also their interpersonal skills and team dynamics involvement. Implement peer feedback systems where team members can nominate and recognize natural leadership within their ranks, highlighting the potential that may not be visible in formal settings.

Tailored Development Opportunities:

Once potential leaders are identified, provide them with development opportunities tailored to their unique skills and career goals. This ensures each potential leader grows in a way that benefits their personal development and the organization's needs. For example, someone innovative may benefit from a project management role launching new initiatives, while someone with strong interpersonal skills may thrive.

Development opportunities should include formal training like leadership workshops as well as practical experiences to apply learned skills. Examples are leading a project, mentoring team members, or shadowing current leaders to understand responsibilities and decision-making. These experiences provide emerging leaders with a deeper understanding of leadership roles and help build confidence to step into those roles effectively.

Mentorship and coaching are indispensable elements in the development of future leaders. Pairing potential leaders with experienced mentors within the organization can accelerate their development by providing them with guidance, insights, and a safe space to discuss challenges and opportunities. Mentors act as role models and advisors, helping mentees navigate the complexities of leadership roles and organizational politics.

Coaching, either by internal leaders or external professionals, can be targeted to polish specific skills such as strategic thinking, communication, or conflict resolution. Coaches work to unlock a potential leader's capabilities, enhancing their performance and preparing them for higher responsibilities. Both mentors and coaches also serve as valuable sounding boards for potential leaders to test their ideas and receive feedback in a constructive and supportive environment.

Empowering Emerging Leaders:

Empowerment is the key to turning potential into actual leadership. This involves trusting emerging leaders with significant responsibilities that test and develop their capabilities. Start by assigning them leadership roles in smaller projects where they can experience leading a team and making decisions, but the stakes are manageable. As their confidence and competence grow, gradually increase their responsibilities and encourage them to take on challenges outside their comfort zones.

It is also crucial to provide emerging leaders with the authority to make decisions regarding their projects. This autonomy fosters a sense of ownership and accountability, essential traits for any leader. However, empowerment also means providing the right support. Ensure that emerging leaders know they have the backing of higher management and can access the resources they need to succeed. Regular check-ins and feedback sessions can help them stay aligned with organizational goals and address any issues they encounter promptly.

In cultivating leadership at every level, you not only ensure a pipeline of capable individuals ready to step into critical roles but also imbue your organization with a vibrant, dynamic energy that propels innovation and growth. By investing in identifying and nurturing potential leaders, you are essentially planting the seeds for your organization's future success, creating a legacy of strong leadership that will sustain your business for years to come.

10.2 Creating a Leadership Development Program: Key Components and Best Practices

Greenleaf Organic Foods, a growing health food company with 120 employees, recognized the importance of developing a strong leadership pipeline to support their expansion plans. To identify and nurture potential leaders, they implemented the following strategies.

They conducted annual performance reviews that assessed not only job-specific skills but also leadership qualities like decision-making, problem-solving, and communication abilities. Employees who demonstrated exceptional leadership potential were nominated for Greenleaf's Leadership Development Program. The program consisted of several key components. Nominated employees were paired with senior leaders as mentors, who provided guidance, shared experiences, and offered coaching on various leadership aspects. Additionally, they participated in leadership training workshops focused on developing competencies like strategic thinking, change management, and emotional intelligence.

Greenleaf also emphasized experiential learning by assigning these high-potential individuals to cross-functional projects or temporary roles in different departments. This exposure broadened their understanding of the business and fostered collaboration across teams. The company created opportunities for these potential leaders to interact with and present to the executive team, increasing their visibility and allowing them to learn from experienced leaders.

Designing Leadership Programs:

Effective leadership development programs typically incorporate a combination of key components like training, practical experiences, mentorship, and coaching. These are tailored to the organization's unique culture, values, and leadership needs. By investing in developing future leaders internally, organizations cultivate a talented and prepared leadership pipeline, ensuring sustainable success and competitive advantage.

Creating and refining a leadership development program is like cultivating a diverse garden, with each plant needing different environments to thrive. An effective program is not just separate training sessions, but a comprehensive, integrated framework designed to cultivate the necessary leadership qualities for the organization's growth and sustainability. Such programs are essential to maintain a robust leadership pipeline and preparedness for future challenges.

Integrating with Strategy:

Regular feedback sessions and personalized development plans were also incorporated to help individuals identify strengths and areas for improvement, ensuring continuous growth and development. By investing in these comprehensive efforts, Greenleaf Organic Foods aimed to build a robust pipeline of future leaders from within, ensuring a seamless transition of leadership roles and maintaining a competitive edge in the rapidly growing health food industry.

A cornerstone of any effective leadership development program is experiential learning. This approach goes beyond traditional classroom learning by immersing potential leaders in real-world challenges and hands-on projects. Experiential learning could involve simulations, role-playing, shadowing current leaders, or leading a team on a small project with real stakes. The key here is to provide experiences that are as close as possible to what leaders will face in their roles.

This not only helps them understand the complexities of leadership but also allows them to apply theoretical knowledge in practical scenarios. Structured feedback helps participants in these programs refine their skills, learn from their mistakes, and better understand their personal leadership styles. This feedback should be timely, specific, and constructive, and should come from credible sources who are invested in the participant's development, such as mentors, peers, and direct reports.

Measuring the Success:

Measuring the success and return on investment (ROI) leadership development programs is crucial to ensure they deliver value and meet organizational needs. This can be challenging since the impact is often seen over a long period. However, both qualitative and quantitative measures can gauge the effectiveness:

Quantitative metrics:

1. Promotion rates of participants vs. non-participants
2. Retention rates of participants
3. Performance improvements in targeted areas

Qualitative assessments:

1. Participant satisfaction
2. Perceived increase in leadership capability
3. Feedback from colleagues and supervisors

It's also beneficial to track participants' career progression over several years to understand the long-term impact on their leadership development. This comprehensive evaluation approach helps validate the program's effectiveness.

Continuously Improving:

Continuously improving leadership development programs cannot remain stagnant if they are to effectively prepare leaders for an ever-changing business landscape. A continuous cycle of improvement is crucial, allowing the content, structure, and delivery methods to adapt based on the latest leadership research, technological advancements, and real-world participant feedback.

Regular program reviews and open dialogue with alumni provide invaluable insights into which aspects were most impactful on their leadership journeys and which areas could be enhanced further. This firsthand perspective guides updates that ensure each new cohort receives a highly relevant, cutting-edge experience that equips them with the mindsets and capabilities to drive meaningful progress.

By intentionally evolving in lockstep with shifting organizational needs, workforce changes, and emerging best practices, these programs avoid becoming outdated or inadequate. Instead, they remain agile and potent experiences that empower leaders to navigate an increasingly dynamic professional reality with vision and skill.

10.3 Leadership and Legacy: Leaving a Mark on Your Organization

The Legacy:

A great leader's impact extends far beyond their day-to-day actions while in a position of authority. It's about the lasting legacy they create - one that influences far more than just current strategies and operations. A leadership legacy shapes the future trajectory of an organization at its core.

Crafting that enduring imprint is a culmination of inspired vision, unwavering commitment, and the profound influence a leader weaves into the very fabric of their organization. It's a spirit that takes root and echoes powerfully even long after that leader has moved on.

This legacy is what separates true visionaries from mere functionaries. It enshrines a leader as someone who fundamentally co-authored the organization's continuing narrative. Who instilled the values, habits of mind, and institutional wisdom that will propel their people to unprecedented heights for generations.

At its essence, a leadership legacy is the gift of foresight, meticulously cultivated over time. It's forging a bridge between the present and the future. Establishing a foundational mindset that will continue inspiring and guiding an organization's path long after its creator has departed. This transcendent impact is what cements a leader's most important contribution - shaping the story that will ultimately outlive them.

Building a Lasting Legacy

Building a lasting legacy through strategic leadership requires deeply engaging with an organization's people and processes. It involves being both a strategic thinker crafting plans for growth and innovation, as well as fostering a culture that sustains those initiatives. For instance, a leader might drive a manufacturing firm towards sustainability by integrating eco-friendly practices.

This strategic shift positions the company as environmentally responsible while also cultivating a culture of innovation and accountability. Over time, this becomes a key part of the leader's enduring legacy, shaping the company's operations and values even after they depart. Strategic leadership creates a positive imprint by aligning the organization's direction with its culture.

Organizational Culture:

Leadership has a profound influence on organizational culture. Culture acts as the fertile soil where a company's strategy and goals take root. Effective leaders understand that their actions, decisions, and approach to challenges directly shape this culture. They set the tone for communication, operations, and innovation within the organization.

By championing transparency, ethics, and employee empowerment, leaders cultivate a positive culture that promotes loyalty, creativity, and efficiency. Over time, this culture becomes a reflection of the leader's values and strategic vision, continuing to guide the organization's path forward even after the leader's tenure. A leader's imprint on the organizational culture has a lasting impact on the company's trajectory.

Case Studies:

Examining case studies of notable leaders who left indelible marks on their organizations provides insights into building a lasting legacy. Consider a tech company leader who transformed it from a struggling player into a global giant. Their approach combined strategic innovations like diversifying products with cultural shifts toward an inclusive, employee-focused environment. These changes drove financial success and built a strong culture of innovation and employee satisfaction.

Another example is a non-profit leader whose community-based strategies expanded the organization's global health impact. Their scalable community engagement model became an enduring legacy for subsequent leaders to build upon. Whether through pioneering strategies or instilling cultures aligned with the organization's mission, impactful leaders create positive footprints that guide their companies' trajectories long after their tenures.

Their examples illustrate how pioneering strategies coupled with fostering mission aligned cultures create positive imprints that guide organizations long after a leader's tenure. As you reflect on these examples, consider how your own leadership can similarly impact your organization.

The legacy you leave as a leader is woven through the daily decisions you make, the values you uphold, and the vision you set forth. It is a combination of your strategic expertise and cultural influence - a lasting imprint that defines not just your tenure but the future direction of your organization. Approach your leadership with the mindset that you are crafting a positive, impactful legacy through your strategic choices and by cultivating an organizational culture aligned with your vision. This legacy will reverberate long after your tenure, influencing the trajectory of the organization for years to come.

Finally, these wide variety of styles underscore the critical role that leadership plays in shaping the culture, performance, and impact of organizations. Leaders set the tone, direction, and expectations for their teams, and have a disproportionate influence on the attitudes, behaviors, and outcomes of their employees. As such, leadership is not just a position or a set of skills, but a profound responsibility and opportunity to make a positive difference in the lives of others and the world at large.

"A leader is one who knows the way, goes the way, and shows the way."

- John C. Maxwell, American author, speaker, and pastor who has written many books on leadership.

Chapter 11
21 Additional Styles

Leadership is a complex and multifaceted concept that has been studied and analyzed from numerous perspectives. There are a wide array of additional leadership approaches that leaders can adopt to effectively guide their teams and organizations. This chapter aims to provide a concise overview of 21 additional leadership styles, each with its unique characteristics, strengths, and potential drawbacks.

The leadership styles covered in these chapters span across various domains, including business, politics, education, and social settings. Some styles prioritize the growth and well-being of followers, while others focus on structure, rules, and rewards. Certain styles rely heavily on the leader's personality and ability to inspire, whereas others emphasize adaptability to different contexts and the follower needs.

It is important to note that no single style is universally effective, and the most successful leaders often demonstrate flexibility in adopting different styles depending on the situation, their followers, and the goals they aim to achieve.

Agile Leadership:

Agile leadership has gained popularity in fast-paced, innovative industries due to its emphasis on adaptability, collaboration, continuous improvement, customer focus, and employee empowerment. While it offers numerous benefits, it also presents challenges that leaders must navigate.

Pros:

- Agile leaders can quickly adapt to the changing market conditions and customer needs.
- Agile leadership promotes high levels of communication and engagement within teams.
- It encourages experimentation, learning, and performance optimization through iteration.
- Agile leadership prioritizes delivering customer value, resulting in increased satisfaction and loyalty.
- It empowers teams to make decisions and develop their skills and autonomy.

Cons:

- Agile leadership can lead to ambiguity in roles and responsibilities, presenting coordination challenges in larger organizations.
- The emphasis on rapid iteration may neglect long-term strategic planning.

- The fast-paced environment can be stressful, potentially leading to decreased job satisfaction if not managed properly.
- Agile leadership requires strong communication, facilitation, and problem-solving skills, necessitating investment in training and development.
- Implementing agile leadership in organizations with traditional management practices can face resistance from employees and stakeholders.

Despite the challenges, agile leadership can drive innovation, engagement, and success in dynamic environments. By using collaboration, continuous improvement, and customer-centricity, agile leaders create a culture that embraces change and delivers value. This requires skillfully balancing flexibility and adaptability with a clear long-term vision and short-term needs.

Agile leaders must be comfortable with ambiguity, empowering their teams to make decisions and learn from failures. They must also be adept at communication, ensuring transparency and alignment across the organization. By breaking down silos, encouraging experimentation, and continuously gathering feedback, agile leaders can quickly respond to changing market conditions and customer needs.

Ultimately, the key to successful agile leadership lies in creating a healthy, productive environment that supports the well-being and growth of employees while driving organizational success in today's rapidly evolving business landscape. With the right mindset, skills, and approach, agile leaders can unlock the full potential of their teams and organizations.

Bureaucratic Leadership:

Bureaucratic leadership, a management style that emphasizes strict adherence to rules, procedures, and hierarchical authority, is often associated with large, complex organizations such as government agencies and traditional corporations.

Pros:

- Ensures consistency and predictability in task performance across the organization
- Provides clear accountability through well-defined roles and responsibilities
- Promotes fairness and impartiality by applying rules and policies uniformly
- Suitable for large organizations requiring standardized processes and centralized decision-making
- Minimizes risk of errors, accidents, or legal liabilities through strict adherence to established procedures

Cons:

- Rigidity and slow adaptation to changing circumstances, stifling innovation and creativity
- Decreased employee motivation and job satisfaction due to strict hierarchy and lack of autonomy
- Slow decision-making process due to complex chain of command and multiple levels of approval
- Communication barriers resulting from formal channels, hindering collaboration and information sharing
- Resistance to change, as existing rules and procedures are often deeply entrenched

While bureaucratic leadership can provide stability, consistency, and scalability for large, complex organizations, it also has significant drawbacks. These include a lack of flexibility, decreased employee motivation, slow decision-making, and resistance to change. In today's rapidly changing business environment, many organizations are shifting towards more agile and adaptive leadership styles to remain competitive and innovative.

However, bureaucratic leadership remains relevant in certain contexts, particularly where standardization, risk management, and compliance are top priorities. Industries such as healthcare, finance, and government often rely on bureaucratic structures to ensure consistent quality, security, and accountability.

The key is to find the right balance between structure and flexibility to meet the specific needs of the organization. By selectively applying bureaucratic principles while also encouraging employee autonomy, creativity, and collaboration, leaders can create a hybrid approach that combines the best of both worlds. This allows organizations to maintain necessary controls and efficiency while also fostering adaptability and growth in an ever-changing business landscape.

Change Leadership:

Change leadership, a management style focused on guiding organizations through significant transformations and adaptations, is becoming increasingly important in today's rapidly evolving business landscape.

Pros:

- Proactively anticipates future challenges and opportunities, developing strategies for success

- Articulates a compelling vision that motivates and inspires employees
- Adapts quickly to new information or changing circumstances
- Empowers teams to take ownership and encourages collaboration across the organization
- Fosters a culture of continuous learning, experimentation, and growth

Cons:

- Faces potential resistance from employees who are comfortable with the status quo or fear change
- May lead to short-term disruptions in productivity and performance during transitions
- Requires significant investments of time, energy, and resources
- Risks failure if changes are poorly planned, inadequately resourced, or misaligned with organizational culture
- Can lead to increased stress levels and the risk of burnout for leaders and employees

Navigating the complexities of today's business environment requires effective change leadership, which presents both opportunities and challenges. Change leaders must proactively drive transformation, inspire employees, and cultivate a culture of adaptability and continuous learning to help their organizations thrive amidst uncertainty. This demands a careful balance between taking risks and delivering meaningful, sustainable results.

Successful change leaders need a clear vision, strong communication skills, and the ability to engage stakeholders at all levels. They must be resilient when facing resistance while demonstrating empathy for those affected by the change. Aligning initiatives with organizational goals, building support, and celebrating short-term wins can maintain momentum and deliver lasting transformations.

However, change leaders must also remain vigilant, continuously assessing progress and adapting strategies as needed to ensure long-term success. Change leadership is challenging but essential for navigating today's dynamic business landscape.

Collaborative Leadership:

Collaborative leadership, a management style that emphasizes teamwork, shared decision-making, and open communication, has gained popularity as organizations recognize the benefits of leveraging diverse perspectives and fostering employee engagement.

Pros:

- Improves decision-making by bringing together individuals with different backgrounds, experiences, and expertise
- Increases employee engagement by giving employees a sense of ownership and empowerment
- Enhances innovation by fostering a culture of idea-sharing and experimentation
- Strengthens relationships and trust through open communication, active listening, and mutual respect
- Improves adaptability by empowering employees to make decisions and take ownership of their work

Cons:

- Slows down decision-making process due to the time required to build consensus and incorporate multiple perspectives
- Potentially leads to conflict and disagreement when bringing together individuals with diverse opinions and backgrounds
- Challenges in assigning clear accountability for decisions and outcomes when responsibilities are shared
- Requires strong facilitation and communication skills, which not all leaders may possess naturally
- Risks groupthink if dissenting opinions are not actively encouraged or if the desire for harmony overrides critical thinking

Collaborative leadership offers numerous benefits, such as harnessing the collective intelligence of team members, driving innovation through diverse perspectives, and fostering engagement by giving employees a sense of ownership in decision-making processes. This approach also presents challenges, including slower decision-making due to the need for consensus, potential for conflict arising from differing viewpoints, and dependence on strong facilitation skills to ensure productive discussions.

Successful collaborative leaders must strike a delicate balance between inclusivity and efficiency. They must establish clear guidelines and processes for decision-making, ensuring that all voices are heard while maintaining a focus on timely outcomes. Developing conflict management and facilitation skills is crucial for mediating disputes and finding common ground among diverse perspectives.

Collaborative leaders must encourage a culture of trust, psychological safety, and mutual respect. By valuing diverse viewpoints, promoting a learning mindset, and encouraging constructive dissent, they can create an environment where team members feel empowered to contribute their best ideas. Despite the challenges, the benefits of leveraging collective intelligence and fostering engagement make collaborative leadership a valuable approach for unlocking the full potential of teams and driving organizational success in today's complex business landscape.

Customer-centric Leadership:

Customer-centric leadership is a management approach that prioritizes the needs, preferences, and experiences of customers in all aspects of organizational decision-making and operations, recognizing that customer satisfaction and loyalty are key drivers of long-term business success and growth.

Pros:

- Increases customer satisfaction and loyalty by consistently prioritizing customer needs and preferences
- Improves brand reputation and differentiation, making organizations appear more responsive, empathetic, and trustworthy
- Enhances innovation and market relevance by identifying emerging trends, unmet needs, and opportunities through customer feedback
- Boosts employee engagement and alignment by emphasizing the importance of customer satisfaction as a core value
- Promotes long-term financial success through strong, loyal customer relationships and consistent value delivery

Cons:

- Pressures short-term financial performance due to investments in customer research, employee training, and process improvements
- Faces resistance to change from employees or stakeholders accustomed to product-centric or sales-driven approaches
- Presents challenges in balancing diverse and sometimes conflicting needs and preferences of different customer segments
- Risks creating a sense of entitlement or unrealistic expectations among customers if not managed carefully
- Relies heavily on the collection, analysis, and interpretation of customer data and feedback, requiring robust infrastructure and analytics capabilities

Customer-centric leadership is a powerful approach for organizations seeking to build strong, loyal customer relationships and achieve long-term success in today's competitive marketplace. By consistently prioritizing customer needs and preferences, customer centric leaders can drive innovation, differentiation, and employee engagement.

Successful customer-centric leaders must navigate challenges such as short-term financial pressures, resistance to change, and the need to balance diverse customer needs while building a culture of customer focus and continuous improvement throughout their organizations. To overcome these obstacles, leaders must possess a clear vision, unwavering commitment, and effective communication skills. They must align organizational goals with customer needs, prioritizing long-term value creation over short-term gains.

By fostering a culture of empathy, innovation, and agility, leaders can inspire their teams to embrace change and continuously adapt to evolving customer expectations. Data-driven insights and regular feedback loops are crucial for making informed decisions and measuring progress. Ultimately, successful customer-centric leaders must lead by example, demonstrating a genuine passion for understanding and serving customers while empowering their teams to do the same.

Entrepreneurial Leadership:

Entrepreneurial leadership is a management approach that focuses on fostering innovation, risk-taking, and proactive problem-solving within organizations, encouraging employees to think and act like entrepreneurs, identify new opportunities, create value, and drive growth and change.

Pros:

- Increases innovation and creativity by encouraging employees to challenge the status quo, take calculated risks, and experiment with new ideas
- Enhances adaptability and resilience by embracing a mindset of continuous learning, iteration, and pivoting
- Improves employee engagement and ownership by empowering employees to take ownership of their work and make decisions
- Enables faster decision-making and execution by reducing bureaucracy and red tape
- Attracts top talent and investors who value innovation, growth, and impact Cons:
- Involves increased risk and uncertainty, exposing the organization to potential volatility and failures

- May lead to burnout and stress among employees due to the fast-paced, high pressure environment
- Can result in a short-term focus and lack of stability, prioritizing rapid growth over long-term sustainability
- Faces resistance from stakeholders and established systems that prefer a more conservative, risk-averse approach
- Presents challenges in scaling and institutionalizing entrepreneurial culture as organizations grow and mature

Entrepreneurial leadership focuses on driving innovation, growth, and change within organizations. By fostering a culture that encourages creativity, calculated risk-taking, and employee empowerment, entrepreneurial leaders can position their organizations for success in today's fast-paced, competitive business environment. They inspire their teams to think like entrepreneurs, constantly seeking new opportunities and finding innovative solutions to challenges.

However, the increased uncertainty and potential for failure can lead to stress and burnout among employees. Additionally, stakeholders may resist the changes and disruptions that often accompany an entrepreneurial approach.

To navigate these challenges, successful entrepreneurial leaders must build resilient, adaptable organizations that can sustain an entrepreneurial mindset and culture over the long term. This requires effective communication, risk management, and support systems for employees. By striking the right balance between innovation and stability, entrepreneurial leaders can harness the power of entrepreneurship to drive lasting success and growth for their organizations.

Environmental Leadership:

Environmental leadership is an increasingly essential approach for organizations seeking to contribute to a more sustainable and resilient future while also driving long-term business success.

Pros:

- Contributes to a more sustainable and resilient future by prioritizing environmental responsibility
- Enhances brand reputation and differentiates the organization from competitors
- Attracts top talent, particularly among younger generations who value purpose driven work
- Drives innovation and efficiency by encouraging the development of eco-friendly products, services, and processes
- Builds stronger relationships with stakeholders, including customers, investors, and communities

Cons:

- Requires significant upfront costs and investments in sustainable technologies, processes, and infrastructure
- Involves navigating complex and evolving environmental regulations, standards, and best practices
- Faces resistance to change from employees, suppliers, or other stakeholders who may be hesitant to adopt new practices
- Depends on external factors, such as consumer behavior, market trends, and policy developments, which can be unpredictable
- Presents challenges in balancing short-term financial pressures with long-term business success.

Environmental leadership is crucial for organizations aiming to create positive environmental impact and drive long-term success. By prioritizing sustainability, ecological responsibility, and stakeholder engagement, leaders can enhance reputation, attract talent, and contribute to a resilient future. However, challenges such as upfront costs, complexity, resistance to change, and external factors must be navigated.

To overcome these challenges, environmental leaders must build a compelling case for sustainability that aligns with their organization's core values. Engaging stakeholders, setting clear goals, and communicating long-term benefits can foster a culture of sustainability that drives innovation and competitive advantage.

Ultimately, environmental leadership requires a strategic, holistic approach balancing environmental stewardship with business success. By integrating environmental considerations into decision-making and overcoming obstacles, leaders can position their organizations for success in an increasingly sustainability-focused world.

Holacratic Leadership:

Holacratic leadership is a management approach that emphasizes self-organization, distributed authority, and adaptive governance within organizations, aiming to replace traditional hierarchical structures with a network of self-managing teams.

Pros:

- Increases agility and adaptability by enabling quick responses to new information, opportunities, or challenges
- Enhances employee autonomy and engagement by

empowering employees to take ownership of their roles and contributions
- Improves collaboration and communication through clear protocols for decision making, conflict resolution, and information sharing
- Reduces bureaucracy and overhead by eliminating layers of management and administrative costs
- Provides scalability and resilience through modular, flexible, and self-healing structures

Cons:

- Involves complexity and a steep learning curve, requiring significant training, coaching, and mindset shifts for employees
- May result in a lack of clear accountability and decision-making, leading to confusion, delays, or inconsistencies
- Creates the potential for interpersonal conflict, power struggles, or blame-shifting among team members
- Presents difficulties in integrating with external stakeholders who are accustomed to traditional hierarchical structures
- Relies heavily on specialized software tools and platforms, creating additional costs, complexities, and dependencies

Holacratic leadership offers a radically different approach to organizing and managing work, prioritizing agility, autonomy, and adaptability. By distributing authority to self-managing teams, holacratic organizations can tap into the collective intelligence and creativity of their employees, fostering innovation and resilience in the face of change.

This approach also presents unique challenges. The complexity of the holacratic system can be difficult to navigate, and accountability gaps may emerge if roles and responsibilities are not clearly defined. Interpersonal tensions can arise as individuals adapt to a more fluid and collaborative work environment. Additionally, holacratic organizations may face integration issues when interacting with external stakeholders who operate under more traditional hierarchical structures.

Successful holacratic leaders must skillfully find their way through these challenges to create the conditions for their teams to thrive. By providing clear frameworks, fostering open communication, and continuously iterating and improving processes, they can unlock the full potential of self-management and adaptability in their organizations.

Innovative Leadership:

Innovative leadership is a management approach that emphasizes creativity, experimentation, and continuous improvement to drive organizational growth and adaptability, encouraging employees to think outside the box, challenge assumptions, and take calculated risks.

Pros:

- Increases competitiveness and market differentiation by constantly seeking new opportunities, technologies, and business models
- Enhances problem-solving and resilience through diverse thinking and a willingness to experiment
- Improves employee engagement and retention by valuing ideas and creating a supportive environment for creativity

- Enables faster learning and adaptation through a culture of experimentation and continuous improvement
- Increases collaboration and cross-functional synergies by breaking down silos and encouraging diverse perspectives

Cons:

- Involves higher risk and uncertainty, requiring effective management of inherent risks and trade-offs associated with experimentation
- Faces resistance to change and disruption from stakeholders who prefer stability and predictability
- Requires significant investments of time, money, and talent, straining organizational resources and budgets
- Risks chaos and lack of focus without clear goals, metrics, and governance structures in place
- Presents challenges in scaling and sustaining innovations over time, necessitating robust systems, processes, and capabilities

Innovative leadership is a profitable approach for organizations seeking to stay ahead in a rapidly changing world. By fostering creativity, experimentation, and continuous learning, innovative leaders help their organizations differentiate themselves, solve complex problems, and create new value.

Challenges include higher risk, resistance to change, resource constraints, and difficulty scaling and sustaining innovation over time. To navigate these challenges, successful innovative leaders must create an environment that supports creative thinking, risk-taking, and learning from failures.

They must communicate the vision and benefits of innovation, rally stakeholder support, and secure resources to bring ideas to life. By building a culture of innovation that permeates all levels of the organization, leaders position their teams to thrive in dynamic and uncertain environments, driving long-term growth and success. Innovative leadership requires skill, vision, and perseverance to overcome obstacles and unlock the power of creativity and continuous improvement.

Knowledge Leadership:

Knowledge leadership is a management approach that emphasizes the creation, sharing, and application of knowledge as a key driver of organizational performance and success, recognizing the critical role of intellectual capital in today's knowledge-based economy.

Pros:

- Enhances organizational learning and adaptation by fostering a culture of continuous learning and knowledge sharing
- Improves problem-solving and decision-making through evidence-based, data driven approaches
- Increases innovation and value creation by encouraging the generation, testing, and refinement of new ideas
- Strengthens collaboration and knowledge sharing by creating structures, processes, and incentives for leveraging intellectual capital
- Attracts and retains top talent by creating a culture of continuous development and knowledge sharing

Cons:

- Risks overemphasizing knowledge acquisition and analysis at the expense of timely decision-making and action
- Presents potential for information overload and inefficiency without proper curation, filtering, and prioritization of knowledge
- Faces challenges in measuring and quantifying knowledge, making it difficult to demonstrate value and impact
- Encounters resistance to knowledge sharing and collaboration due to concerns about intellectual property, trust, or lack of incentives
- Requires strategies for capturing, codifying, and refreshing critical knowledge assets to prevent loss and obsolescence over time

Knowledge leadership offers a unique outlook for organizations seeking to thrive in today's knowledge-based economy. By prioritizing learning, collaboration, and innovation, knowledge leaders help teams continuously grow, adapt, and create value. They encourage knowledge sharing, experimentation, and applying insights to drive success.

Leaders must balance knowledge acquisition with timely action, manage information overload, measure intangible assets, overcome resistance to sharing, and prevent knowledge loss and obsolescence.

Successful knowledge leaders create a culture that values and rewards knowledge sharing, provides tools and processes for collaboration, and aligns knowledge management with strategic goals. By demonstrating the value of knowledge leadership and engaging employees, leaders can tap into their organization's collective intelligence, driving sustainable growth and innovation. Knowledge leadership requires a strategic, holistic approach to leveraging knowledge as a competitive advantage.

Lean Leadership:

Lean leadership is a management approach that focuses on eliminating waste, continuously improving processes, and maximizing customer value. Rooted in lean manufacturing principles, it has been adopted across many industries.

Pros

- Increases efficiency and productivity by streamlining processes and cutting out non-value-added activities
- Enhances customer focus by aligning all efforts around delivering customer value
- Drives continuous improvement and problem-solving using methods like root cause analysis
- Empowers and engages employees by enabling them to make improvements and decisions

Cons

- Can cause short-term disruption and employee resistance when first implemented
- May overemphasize efficiency at the expense of innovation and creative risk taking
- Challenging to sustain lean culture over the long-term without ongoing leadership commitment
- Can risk employee burnout and stress if problem-solving demands are not balanced with support

- Requires active collaboration with suppliers and customers which can be difficult in some industries

While lean leadership offers significant benefits centering around efficiency, quality, and engagement, it also poses challenges in managing change, balancing priorities, and sustaining momentum. By focusing on continuous improvement, waste reduction, and value creation, lean leaders can streamline processes, enhance quality, and boost productivity. Lean principles also emphasize employee empowerment and collaboration, leading to increased job satisfaction and motivation.

Employees may resist new ways of working, and balancing cost reduction, quality improvement, and customer satisfaction can be challenging. Sustaining momentum and ensuring long-term adoption of lean practices requires ongoing commitment and resources.

Successful lean leaders must provide training and support, encourage experimentation, and recognize lean behaviors. With committed and capable lean leadership, organizations can reap the full value of lean thinking and drive long-term success.

Performance Leadership:

Performance leadership is a results-oriented approach that sets high expectations, provides support and resources, and holds employees accountable for achieving specific, measurable goals. It aims to drive individual and organizational performance improvement.

Pros

- Provides clarity of goals and expectations so employees understand what success looks like

- Focuses on delivering results and accountability to drive a culture of excellence
- Emphasizes data-driven, evidence-based decision making to remove bias and subjectivity
- Recognizes and rewards high performance to motivate employees to excel
- Continuously develops employees' skills through feedback, coaching and development opportunities

Cons

- May encourage short-term thinking and risk aversion at the expense of long-term strategy
- Can create stress and burnout due to constant pressure to achieve challenging targets
- Risks overemphasizing individual performance over collaboration and teamwork
- Struggles to measure and value intangible, long-term outcomes like engagement and loyalty
- Could tempt unethical behavior or gaming the system in a high-stakes, results driven culture

Performance leadership is a powerful approach for driving results, accountability, and continuous improvement within organizations. By setting clear goals, tracking key performance metrics, and rewarding achievement, performance leaders can motivate their teams to excel and deliver outstanding outcomes. This approach creates a culture of ownership and responsibility, where everyone understands their role in contributing to the organization's success.

Performance leadership also requires carefully balancing the pursuit of results with long-term sustainability, ethical considerations, and employee well-being. An excessive focus on short-term performance can lead to burnout, corner-cutting, and a neglect of important non-financial measures. Successful performance leaders must combine a strong results orientation with emotional intelligence skills such as empathy, communication, and the ability to inspire and engage their teams.

These leaders must set realistic and achievable goals, provide regular feedback and coaching, and create an environment that supports learning and growth. They must also foster open communication, trust, and collaboration within their teams, recognizing that sustainable high performance is a collective effort.

Risk Leadership:

Risk leadership is a management approach focused on identifying, assessing and managing risks to protect and create organizational value. It recognizes risk is inherent in business and proactively addresses it.

Pros

- Proactively identifies and mitigates potential risks through assessments, planning and testing
- Improves decision-making by weighing the risks and rewards to inform strategic resource allocation
- Enhances organizational resilience to weather shocks and emerge stronger from disruptions
- Increases stakeholder confidence by demonstrating commitment to risk management and transparency
- Ensures compliance with complex legal/regulatory requirements to avoid penalties and liabilities

Cons

- May lead to risk aversion and missed opportunities if too focused on minimizing downside risks
- Struggles to quantify and communicate complex risks into clear, actionable insights from non-experts
- Requires significant investment in risk management talent, processes and technology which can be costly
- Risks creating silos if risk management is not well-integrated across different business functions
- Challenges leaders to balance short-term tactical risks with long-term strategic risks

Risk leadership is critical for navigating complex, uncertain business environments. By proactively identifying, assessing, and managing risks, leaders help organizations make informed decisions, build resilience, and drive long-term value creation. They foster a culture of risk awareness and accountability, integrating risk considerations into strategic planning and daily operations.

However, risk leadership must balance risk mitigation with openness to opportunities, as overemphasis on risk avoidance can stifle innovation and growth. Effective risk leaders apply both art and science, leveraging data and analytics while relying on experience and judgment to navigate ambiguity.

Risk leaders must engage stakeholders across the enterprise to build shared understanding of key risks and mitigation strategies. By embracing risk as an opportunity to strengthen the organization, they help avoid costly mistakes, seize opportunities, and build agility and resilience. Risk leadership is a strategic enabler, fostering informed risk taking and continuous learning.

Situational Leadership:

Situational leadership is a flexible management style that adapts to the unique needs and characteristics of each team member and situation. This approach recognizes that there is no one-size-fits-all leadership method, and effective leaders must be able to adjust their behavior based on the context.

Pros:

- Tailored approach to individual development
- Increased adaptability and responsiveness to change
- Improved communication and collaboration
- Enhanced problem-solving and decision-making
- Development of leadership skills at all levels

Cons:

- Requires significant time and effort to implement effectively
- May be perceived as inconsistent or unfair
- Challenging to scale in larger organizations
- Requires a high level of emotional intelligence and adaptability
- May not be appropriate in all situations or cultures

Situational leadership can drive engagement, collaboration, and continuous learning within organizations. By tailoring their leadership style to the needs and readiness of each individual team member, situational leaders can provide the right level of direction, support, and coaching to help employees develop and succeed. This adaptable approach fosters a culture of trust, empowerment, and growth, as leaders demonstrate their commitment to meeting the unique needs of each person.

However, the time and effort required to assess individual needs and adapt one's leadership style can be significant, particularly in larger teams. There is also a risk of inconsistency if leaders struggle to apply the approach fairly and effectively across all team members. Scalability can be an issue, as the individualized nature of situational leadership may be more difficult to implement in larger organizations.

Situational leadership requires a high level of emotional intelligence and interpersonal skills. Leaders must be adept at reading and responding to the emotions, motivations, and capabilities of each team member, while also maintaining a clear vision and direction for the team as a whole.

Situational leaders must create a culture of trust, transparency, and continuous improvement. They must invest time in getting to know each team member, regularly assessing their needs and progress, and providing timely and constructive feedback. They must also be willing to adapt their approach as circumstances change, while maintaining consistency in their overall leadership philosophy and values.

Supply Chain Leadership:

Supply Chain leadership involves optimizing the flow of goods, services, and information from suppliers to customers, with the goal of creating value and competitive advantage. This approach recognizes the pivotal role of effective supply chain management in today's global business landscape.

Pros:

- Improved efficiency and cost savings
- Enhanced customer satisfaction and loyalty

- Greater agility and resilience to disruptions
- Improved collaboration and partnerships
- Competitive advantage through supply chain excellence

Cons:

- Complexity and interdependence of supply chain systems
- Difficulty aligning incentives across the supply chain
- Dependence on technology and data management
- Vulnerability to external risks and disruptions
- Need for continuous improvement and innovation

Supply chain leadership offers significant advantages by streamlining operations, enhancing customer service, building resilience, fostering collaboration, and driving competitive edge. By optimizing processes, leveraging technology, and building strong partnerships, supply chain leaders can reduce costs, improve efficiency, and deliver superior value to customers. They can also help their organizations navigate disruptions and adapt to changing market conditions.

Supply chain leadership also has challenges related to system complexity, aligning objectives, technology dependence, external risks, and the need for ongoing innovation. Effective supply chain leaders must work through these negatives while cultivating a culture of excellence, agility, and adaptability throughout the supply chain.

This requires strong communication, collaboration, and change management skills, as well as a deep understanding of supply chain management. Leaders must balance short term operational demands with long-term strategic objectives, making data-driven decisions that optimize performance and create sustainable value. By combining technical expertise with visionary leadership, supply chain leaders can help their organizations thrive in an increasingly complex and competitive world.

Strategic Leadership:

Strategic leadership focuses on setting long-term vision, direction, and goals of an organization, while aligning resources and actions to achieve those objectives. This approach is concerned with positioning the company for success in a complex and everchanging business landscape.

Pros:

- Clear direction and purpose
- Adaptability and agility in the face of change
- Effective resource allocation and decision-making
- Talent development and succession planning
- Stakeholder engagement and reputation management

Cons:

- Potential over-emphasis on long-term at the expense of short-term
- Difficulty translating vision into actionable plans
- Resistance to change and risk aversion
- Dependence on external factors and assumptions
- Potential for hubris and overconfidence

Strategic leadership enables organizations to create long-term value, adapt to changes, and build sustainable competitive advantages. By setting a compelling vision, making informed decisions, developing talent, and engaging stakeholders, strategic leaders can guide their companies toward success. They anticipate future trends, identify opportunities, and allocate resources to capitalize on them, while also fostering a culture of innovation and continuous improvement.

This approach also carries risks that leaders must navigate skillfully. An excessive focus on long-term strategy can lead to neglecting short-term priorities and operational effectiveness. Executing the vision can be challenging, particularly if it requires significant changes to the organization's culture, structure, or processes. Strategic leaders may face resistance from employees, shareholders, or other stakeholders who are comfortable with the status quo or skeptical of the new direction.

Strategic leadership often relies on assumptions about the future that may prove inaccurate or incomplete. Overconfidence in one's vision and abilities can lead to underestimating risks, ignoring warning signs, or failing to adapt to changing circumstances.

Strategic leaders must balance vision with execution, short-term and long-term priorities, and boldness and humility. They must engage in continuous learning, seeking out diverse perspectives and adapting their strategies as needed. They must also build strong teams, empower others to lead, and foster a culture of accountability and agility. This style requires a combination of foresight, decisiveness, adaptability, and interpersonal skills. By setting a clear direction, aligning resources, and inspiring others to follow, strategic leaders can help their organizations navigate uncertainty, seize opportunities, and create lasting value.

Team-based Leadership:

Team-based leadership emphasizes collaboration, shared responsibility, and collective decision-making within teams or groups. This approach recognizes that the best outcomes often emerge when diverse individuals work together toward a common goal, leveraging their unique skills and perspectives.

Pros:

- Increased creativity and innovation
- Enhanced problem-solving and decision-making
- Greater employee engagement and ownership
- Improved communication and collaboration
- Leadership development and succession planning

Cons:

- Potential for conflict and dysfunction
- Slower decision-making and execution
- Diffusion of accountability and ownership
- Depending on team dynamics and composition
- Difficulty scaling and integrating with broader organizational structures

Team-based leadership is a powerful approach that drives innovation, collaboration, and engagement by empowering individuals to work together toward shared goals. By tapping into the collective intelligence and creativity of teams, this approach can build more adaptive and resilient organizations. Team-based leaders foster a culture of trust, psychological safety, and open communication, enabling team members to share ideas, take risks, and learn from each other.

Potential conflicts may arise among team members with different personalities, working styles, or priorities. Decision-making can be slower, as teams may need more time to build consensus and align their efforts. Accountability may be diffused, making it harder to identify and address performance issues.

The success of team-based leadership is highly dependent on team dynamics, which can be influenced by factors such as team composition, size, and stage of development.

Scaling team-based approaches across larger organizations can also be challenging, as it requires consistent practices, structures, and support systems.

Effective team-based leaders must create the conditions for teams to thrive while ensuring alignment with broader organizational strategies and goals. This involves providing clear direction and expectations, fostering a culture of psychological safety and inclusion, coaching teams to develop their capabilities, and facilitating effective communication and collaboration across boundaries.

When implemented well, team-based leadership can be a key driver of success in an increasingly complex business landscape. By leveraging the diverse skills, perspectives, and experiences of team members, organizations can respond more nimbly to challenges, innovate more effectively, and create greater value for all stakeholders.

Transactional Leadership:

Transactional leadership is a management style that focuses on the exchange of rewards and punishments to motivate employees and achieve organizational goals. This approach emphasizes clear expectations, performance monitoring, and contingent rewards or consequences based on results.

Pros:

- Clarity of expectations and goals
- Efficiency and productivity
- Fairness and consistency
- Motivation and accountability
- Scalability and ability to replicate

Cons:

- Short-term focus and lack of vision
- Lack of employee development and engagement
- Stifling creativity and risk-taking
- Dependence on external motivation
- Potential for abuse and unethical behavior

Transactional leadership can be effective for driving short-term results and accountability in stable environments. By setting clear goals, providing incentives, and ensuring fairness, transactional leaders can motivate employees to achieve specific objectives. This approach establishes a clear framework for performance expectations and rewards, which can be particularly useful in roles that require adherence to standards or processes.

However, its narrow focus on short-term goals can neglect employee development, stifle innovation, and create an overdependence on external rewards. When taken to extremes, transactional leadership may even lead to unethical behavior, as employees prioritize personal gains over organizational values.

To be truly effective, transactional leadership should be

balanced with other styles that emphasize vision, empowerment, and long-term growth. Transformational, servant, and situational leadership approaches can complement transactional elements by inspiring employees, fostering their development, and adapting to changing needs.

Used judiciously and in combination with other approaches, transactional leadership can be a valuable tool for ensuring accountability and driving results. However, when overused or misused, it can undermine an organization's culture, engagement, and long term success. The key is to find the right balance and apply transactional principles in a way that supports, rather than detracts from, the organization's overall mission and values.

Transformational Leadership:

Transformational leadership inspires and motivates employees to achieve exceptional results by creating a shared vision, fostering creativity, and promoting personal and professional growth. This approach emphasizes vision, charisma, intellectual stimulation, and individualized consideration.

Pros:

- Visionary and inspiring
- Empowering and developmentally focused
- Intellectually stimulating and innovative
- Emotionally intelligent and supportive
- Adaptable and future-oriented

Cons:

- Dependence on leader's personality and charisma
- Potential for narcissism and abuse of power

- Difficulty balancing vision with execution
- Resistance to change and burnout
- Overemphasis on individual leader vs. team

Transformational leadership can drive innovation, engagement, and performance by articulating a compelling vision, empowering employees, fostering intellectual growth, and navigating change. By inspiring followers to transcend self-interest and embrace a shared purpose, transformational leaders can unlock extraordinary potential and create lasting value.

This approach also carries risks, such as overreliance on the leader's charisma, potential for abuse of power, struggles in translating vision into execution, resistance to change from stakeholders, and an overemphasis on the individual leader rather than the team or system.

For sustainable success, transformational leadership should be balanced with approaches that emphasize teamwork, accountability, operational excellence, and succession planning. Transformational elements should be integrated with transactional, servant, and situational leadership styles to ensure a holistic and adaptable approach.

When used appropriately alongside other styles, transformational leadership can catalyze positive change and drive remarkable results. However, when misused or overused, it can undermine long-term organizational health and success. The key is to harness the power of transformational leadership while mitigating its risks and balancing it with complementary approaches that foster resilience, sustainability, and shared ownership of the organization's future.

Quality Leadership:

Quality leadership emphasizes continuous improvement, customer satisfaction, and data-driven decision-making to achieve excellence in products, services, and processes. This approach, rooted in total quality management principles, engages all employees in the pursuit of quality.

Pros:

- Customer focus and satisfaction
- Continuous improvement and learning
- Data-driven decision-making
- Employee engagement and empowerment
- Systemic and holistic thinking

Cons:

- Time and resource intensity
- Resistance to change and bureaucracy
- Overemphasis on process vs. people
- Difficulty measuring and sustaining quality
- Potential for perfectionism and risk aversion

Quality leadership drives customer satisfaction, continuous improvement, and operational excellence by prioritizing customer needs, using data for decisions, engaging employees, and taking a systemic view. This approach can enhance efficiency, reduce errors, and create a culture of quality throughout the organization.

Challenges include a resource intensity required to implement and maintain quality systems, resistance to change from employees, potential bureaucracy and rigidity, neglecting human factors in favor of process, difficulties in measuring intangible aspects of quality, and the risk of perfectionism or risk aversion stifling innovation. To be effective, quality leadership must balance process and people, and be used in combination with approaches that emphasize innovation, agility, and human-centered design. Quality leaders must also cultivate a mindset of continuous learning, adaptation, and employee empowerment.

When implemented well, quality leadership provides a foundation for long-term success, customer loyalty, and sustainable performance. However, when overused or misused, it can create rigidity, limit creativity, and undermine its own goals. The key is to integrate quality principles with other leadership approaches in a way that enhances, rather than constrains, the organization's ability to deliver value to its stakeholders.

Virtual Leadership:

Virtual leadership involves leading and coordinating geographically dispersed teams that rely on technology for communication and collaboration. This approach has grown amid the shift to remote work and digital operations.

Pros:

- Flexibility and work-life balance
- Cost savings and efficiency
- Innovation and agility
- Empowerment and accountability
- Resilience and business continuity

Cons:

- Communication and collaboration challenges
- Technology and infrastructure dependencies

- Difficulty building and maintaining culture
- Blurred boundaries and burnout risk
- Cybersecurity and data privacy risks

Virtual leadership offers opportunities for flexibility, cost savings, innovation, empowerment, and resilience by enabling remote, tech-enabled collaboration. By leveraging digital tools and platforms, virtual leaders can connect diverse talent, foster asynchronous work, and drive results across boundaries.

Challenges include technology dependencies, culture building, work-life balance, and cybersecurity risks. Without face-to-face interaction, misunderstandings can arise, and building trust and rapport can be more difficult. Heavy reliance on technology can create vulnerabilities and inequities. Maintaining a strong culture and work-life boundaries can also be challenging in an "always-on" digital environment.

Effective virtual leaders must intentionally foster trust, collaboration, and purpose within their teams. They need to adapt their communication and leadership style to the needs of remote workers, leveraging both synchronous and asynchronous channels. They must also prioritize cybersecurity, digital inclusion, and employee wellbeing.

When used appropriately alongside other leadership approaches, virtual leadership can drive performance and engagement in the digital workplace. But when overused or misused, it risks creating disconnection, burnout, and undermining its intended advantages. Balancing the pros and cons through skilled, adaptable, and human-centric leadership is crucial for sustainable success in the virtual realm.

Chapter 12
Determine Your Style *(Avoid Pitfalls)* DCS5 Personality Assessments

12.1 What To Avoid

A few things a great leader would 'never' do….

Remember: Nobody's Perfect!

1. **Micromanaging:** Excessive control and attention to minor details, limiting employee autonomy, creativity, and trust, often leading to decreased morale and productivity in the workplace.
2. **Taking Credit for Others' Work:** Good leaders recognize and celebrate the contributions of their team members rather than claiming credit for achievements that belong to the team.
3. **Avoiding Feedback:** Good leaders actively seek

feedback from their team members and are open to constructive criticism and suggestions for improvement.
4. **Being Inflexible:** Good leaders are adaptable and willing to adjust their plans and strategies based on changing circumstances and feedback from stakeholders.
5. **Ignoring Personal Development:** Good leaders prioritize their own continuous learning and development, recognizing that personal growth contributes to leadership effectiveness.
6. Playing Favorites: Good leaders treat all team members fairly and avoid showing favoritism or bias toward specific individuals or groups.
7. **Being Closed-Minded:** Good leaders maintain an open mind and consider different perspectives and ideas, fostering a culture of innovation and creativity within their teams.
8. **Avoiding Difficult Conversations:** Good leaders address issues and conflicts directly and constructively, avoiding avoidance or procrastination when it comes to challenging conversations.
9. **Setting Unrealistic Expectations:** Good leaders set achievable goals and expectations for their team members, avoiding placing undue pressure or creating an environment of constant stress.
10. **Lacking Transparency:** Good leaders communicate openly and transparently with their team members, sharing relevant information and insights to foster trust and collaboration.
11. **Playing the Blame Game:** Good leaders take responsibility for mistakes and failures instead of

blaming others, fostering a culture of accountability and learning from setbacks.

12. **Being Overly Controlling:** Good leaders delegate tasks and responsibilities effectively, allowing team members the autonomy to make decisions within their areas of expertise.

13. **Neglecting Communication:** Good leaders prioritize clear and consistent communication, ensuring that team members are informed and aligned with organizational goals and strategies.

14. **Being Inaccessible:** Good leaders are approachable and accessible to their team members, encouraging open dialogue and providing support when needed.

15. **Promoting Toxic Competition:** Good leaders promote a collaborative and supportive environment, discouraging unhealthy competition and focusing on collective success rather than individual rivalries.

16. **Ignoring Employee Well-being:** Good leaders prioritize the well-being and work-life balance of their team members, recognizing the importance of mental and physical health for productivity and morale.

17. **Overlooking Diversity and Inclusion:** Good leaders value diversity and inclusion, creating opportunities for all team members to contribute and thrive regardless of background or identity.

18. **Making Rash Decisions:** Good leaders take the time to gather information, consider alternatives, and consult with stakeholders before making important decisions, avoiding impulsivity or recklessness.

19. **Neglecting Recognition and Appreciation:** Good leaders regularly acknowledge and appreciate the efforts

and achievements of their team members, boosting morale and motivation.

20. **Losing Sight of the Big Picture:** Good leaders maintain a strategic focus on long-term goals and organizational vision, avoiding distractions and staying aligned with overarching objectives.

12.2 DCS5 Personality Assessment: Time to Take the Survey

The purpose of leadership style surveys is to help individuals assess and understand their own leadership tendencies, preferences, and behaviors. By responding to a series of statements related to various leadership approaches, participants can gain insights into their dominant leadership style and identify areas for personal and professional development.

Determining your leadership style involves self-reflection, feedback from others, and observation of your own behavior in various leadership situations. After completing the following survey, review your responses and the identified leadership styles to gain insights into your dominant leadership style and areas for further development or refinement. Additional information on each style is given in previous chapters.

This portion of the *DCS5* covers five of the most identifiable leadership styles:

1. **Servant Leadership:** Focuses on serving and empowering others, prioritizing the growth and well-being of team members.
2. **Democratic Leadership:** Emphasizes participation, collaboration, and consensus building in decision-

making processes.
3. **Authoritarian Leadership:** Concentrates power and decision-making authority with the leader, expecting obedience and adherence to rules.
4. **Laissez-faire Leadership:** Characterized by a hands-off approach, providing team members with significant autonomy and minimal guidance.
5. **Charismatic Leadership:** Relies on the leader's personal charm, vision, and ability to inspire and motivate others.

Scoring: For each survey, participants rate their level of agreement with each statement on a scale from 1 to 5, where: 1 = Strongly Disagree, 2 = Disagree, 3 = Neutral, 4 = Agree, 5 = Strongly Agree.

To calculate the score for each leadership style, participants add up the ratings for all statements within that particular survey. A higher total score indicates a stronger alignment with that specific leadership style.

It is important to note that individuals may exhibit characteristics of multiple leadership styles, and scores should be interpreted as tendencies rather than absolute classifications. The insights gained from these surveys can help leaders and stakeholders recognize their strengths, identify potential blind spots, and develop a more well-rounded and effective leadership approach based on their unique context and goals.

12.3 Servant Leadership

1. Serving others is what I believe to be a leader's primary role.

1	2	3	4	5
Strongly Disagree	Disagree	Neutral	Agree	Strongly Agree

2. My team members' well-being and development take precedence over my personal goals.

1	2	3	4	5
Strongly Disagree	Disagree	Neutral	Agree	Strongly Agree

3. I consider collaboration and teamwork to be crucial for effective leadership.

1	2	3	4	5
Strongly Disagree	Disagree	Neutral	Agree	Strongly Agree

4. Leaders should actively listen to and empathize with the concerns of their team members.

1	2	3	4	5
Strongly Disagree	Disagree	Neutral	Agree	Strongly Agree

5. Leadership, in my view, is a way to serve and support the growth and development of others.

1	2	3	4	5
Strongly Disagree	Disagree	Neutral	Agree	Strongly Agree

6. To improve my leadership approach, I regularly seek and use feedback from team members.

1	2	3	4	5
Strongly Disagree	Disagree	Neutral	Agree	Strongly Agree

7. I value team members' input and actively involve them in decision-making processes.

1	2	3	4	5
Strongly Disagree	Disagree	Neutral	Agree	Strongly Agree

8. Serving the needs of others is more important to me than asserting authority or control.

1	2	3	4	5
Strongly Disagree	Disagree	Neutral	Agree	Strongly Agree

9. I hold myself accountable for the success and well-being of my team members.

1	2	3	4	5
Strongly Disagree	Disagree	Neutral	Agree	Strongly Agree

10. Within my team, I foster a culture of humility, empathy, and inclusivity.

1	2	3	4	5
Strongly Disagree	Disagree	Neutral	Agree	Strongly Agree

11. My clear vision focuses on serving others and making a positive impact.

1	2	3	4	5
Strongly Disagree	Disagree	Neutral	Agree	Strongly Agree

12. Long-term goals and sustainability are more important to me than short-term gains.

1	2	3	4	5
Strongly Disagree	Disagree	Neutral	Agree	Strongly Agree

13. I measure the success of leadership by the growth and well-being of team members.

1	2	3	4	5
Strongly Disagree	Disagree	Neutral	Agree	Strongly Agree

14. I empower team members to take initiative and make decisions within their roles.

1	2	3	4	5
Strongly Disagree	Disagree	Neutral	Agree	Strongly Agree

15. Building strong relationships and trust with team members is one of my top priorities.

1	2	3	4	5
Strongly Disagree	Disagree	Neutral	Agree	Strongly Agree

16. I frequently reflect on my leadership style and look for ways to improve myself.

1	2	3	4	5
Strongly Disagree	Disagree	Neutral	Agree	Strongly Agree

17. Within my team, I promote a culture of learning and development.

1	2	3	4	5
Strongly Disagree	Disagree	Neutral	Agree	Strongly Agree

18. To understand my team members' needs and concerns, I actively seek their feedback.

1	2	3	4	5
Strongly Disagree	Disagree	Neutral	Agree	Strongly Agree

19. I encourage team members to take ownership and responsibility.

1	2	3	4	5
Strongly Disagree	Disagree	Neutral	Agree	Strongly Agree

20. The growth and development of team members is a key aspect of my leadership role.

1	2	3	4	5
Strongly Disagree	Disagree	Neutral	Agree	Strongly Agree

21. Involving team members in decision-making, in my opinion, leads to better outcomes.

1	2	3	4	5
Strongly Disagree	Disagree	Neutral	Agree	Strongly Agree

22. Before making decisions, I seek input and ideas from team members.

1	2	3	4	5
Strongly Disagree	Disagree	Neutral	Agree	Strongly Agree

23. In decision-making processes, I value consensus and collaboration.

1	2	3	4	5
Strongly Disagree	Disagree	Neutral	Agree	Strongly Agree

24. I believe every team member should have a say in decisions that affect them.

1	2	3	4	5
Strongly Disagree	Disagree	Neutral	Agree	Strongly Agree

25. When it comes to decision-making, I trust the expertise and judgment of my team members.

1	2	3	4	5
Strongly Disagree	Disagree	Neutral	Agree	Strongly Agree

26. I am open and transparent with my team members about decisions and plans.

1	2	3	4	5
Strongly Disagree	Disagree	Neutral	Agree	Strongly Agree

27. I encourage open dialogue and feedback from team members.

1	2	3	4	5
Strongly Disagree	Disagree	Neutral	Agree	Strongly Agree

28. I strive to ensure information is shared equally among team members.

1	2	3	4	5
Strongly Disagree	Disagree	Neutral	Agree	Strongly Agree

29. In my view, clear communication builds trust and fosters collaboration.

1	2	3	4	5
Strongly Disagree	Disagree	Neutral	Agree	Strongly Agree

30. I welcome feedback and suggestions from team members about team processes and decisions.

1	2	3	4	5
Strongly Disagree	Disagree	Neutral	Agree	Strongly Agree

31. I empower team members to take initiative and make decisions within their roles.

1	2	3	4	5
Strongly Disagree	Disagree	Neutral	Agree	Strongly Agree

32. I delegate tasks and responsibilities based on team members' skills and interests.

1	2	3	4	5
Strongly Disagree	Disagree	Neutral	Agree	Strongly Agree

33. I provide opportunities for team members to contribute ideas and suggestions for improvement.

1	2	3	4	5
Strongly Disagree	Disagree	Neutral	Agree	Strongly Agree

34. I encourage autonomy and self-management among team members.

1	2	3	4	5
Strongly Disagree	Disagree	Neutral	Agree	Strongly Agree

35. Shared leadership and collective decision-making, in my view, lead to a stronger team.

1	2	3	4	5
Strongly Disagree	Disagree	Neutral	Agree	Strongly Agree

36. I regularly provide feedback and recognition to team members for their contributions.

1	2	3	4	5
Strongly Disagree	Disagree	Neutral	Agree	Strongly Agree

37. I encourage peer feedback and recognition within the team.

1	2	3	4	5
Strongly Disagree	Disagree	Neutral	Agree	Strongly Agree

38. I listen to and act upon feedback from team members about team processes and dynamics.

1	2	3	4	5
Strongly Disagree	Disagree	Neutral	Agree	Strongly Agree

39. Recognizing individual and team achievements, in my opinion, is important for morale and motivation.

1	2	3	4	5
Strongly Disagree	Disagree	Neutral	Agree	Strongly Agree

40. I involve team members in setting goals and expectations for their own performance.

1	2	3	4	5
Strongly Disagree	Disagree	Neutral	Agree	Strongly Agree

Servant Leadership

Totals

Strongly Disagree   1 _____

Disagree   2 _____

Neutral   3 _____

Agree   4 _____

Strongly Agree   5 _____

Total

Servant Personality Assessment   _____

12.4 Democratic Leadership

1. I believe in involving team members in the decision-making process.

1	2	3	4	5
Strongly Disagree	Disagree	Neutral	Agree	Strongly Agree

2. I encourage open communication and dialogue among team members.

1	2	3	4	5
Strongly Disagree	Disagree	Neutral	Agree	Strongly Agree

3. I value the opinions and perspectives of all team members.

1	2	3	4	5
Strongly Disagree	Disagree	Neutral	Agree	Strongly Agree

4. I strive to create a collaborative and inclusive work environment.

1	2	3	4	5
Strongly Disagree	Disagree	Neutral	Agree	Strongly Agree

5. I believe that consensus-building is an important aspect of effective leadership.

1	2	3	4	5
Strongly Disagree	Disagree	Neutral	Agree	Strongly Agree

6. I encourage team members to take ownership of their work and responsibilities.

1	2	3	4	5
Strongly Disagree	Disagree	Neutral	Agree	Strongly Agree

7. I believe in delegating tasks and authority to team members when appropriate.

1	2	3	4	5
Strongly Disagree	Disagree	Neutral	Agree	Strongly Agree

8. I actively seek feedback from team members to improve my leadership.

1	2	3	4	5
Strongly Disagree	Disagree	Neutral	Agree	Strongly Agree

9. I believe in fostering a culture of trust and mutual respect within the team.

1	2	3	4	5
Strongly Disagree	Disagree	Neutral	Agree	Strongly Agree

10. I encourage team members to share their ideas and suggestions openly.

1	2	3	4	5
Strongly Disagree	Disagree	Neutral	Agree	Strongly Agree

11. I believe in making decisions based on the collective wisdom of the team.

1	2	3	4	5
Strongly Disagree	Disagree	Neutral	Agree	Strongly Agree

12. I strive to create an environment where team members feel empowered to take initiative.

1	2	3	4	5
Strongly Disagree	Disagree	Neutral	Agree	Strongly Agree

13. I believe in the importance of transparency and information sharing within the team.

1	2	3	4	5
Strongly Disagree	Disagree	Neutral	Agree	Strongly Agree

14. I encourage team members to develop their skills and expertise.

1	2	3	4	5
Strongly Disagree	Disagree	Neutral	Agree	Strongly Agree

15. I believe in the value of diverse perspectives and experiences within the team.

1	2	3	4	5
Strongly Disagree	Disagree	Neutral	Agree	Strongly Agree

16. I strive to create a safe space for team members to express their concerns and ideas.

1	2	3	4	5
Strongly Disagree	Disagree	Neutral	Agree	Strongly Agree

17. I believe in the importance of recognizing and celebrating team achievements.

1	2	3	4	5
Strongly Disagree	Disagree	Neutral	Agree	Strongly Agree

18. I encourage team members to take calculated risks and learn from their mistakes.

1	2	3	4	5
Strongly Disagree	Disagree	Neutral	Agree	Strongly Agree

19. I believe in the power of collaboration and teamwork to achieve common goals.

1	2	3	4	5
Strongly Disagree	Disagree	Neutral	Agree	Strongly Agree

20. I strive to create an environment where team members feel valued and appreciated.

1	2	3	4	5
Strongly Disagree	Disagree	Neutral	Agree	Strongly Agree

21. I believe in the importance of setting clear expectations and goals for the team.

1	2	3	4	5
Strongly Disagree	Disagree	Neutral	Agree	Strongly Agree

22. I encourage team members to take on leadership roles and responsibilities when appropriate.

1	2	3	4	5
Strongly Disagree	Disagree	Neutral	Agree	Strongly Agree

23. I believe in the value of constructive feedback and continuous improvement.

1	2	3	4	5
Strongly Disagree	Disagree	Neutral	Agree	Strongly Agree

24. I strive to create an environment where team members feel comfortable expressing dissenting opinions.

1	2	3	4	5
Strongly Disagree	Disagree	Neutral	Agree	Strongly Agree

25. I believe in the importance of fostering a sense of shared purpose and vision within the team.

1	2	3	4	5
Strongly Disagree	Disagree	Neutral	Agree	Strongly Agree

26. I encourage team members to actively participate in problem-solving and decision making.

1	2	3	4	5
Strongly Disagree	Disagree	Neutral	Agree	Strongly Agree

27. I believe in the value of open and honest communication, even when it's difficult.

1	2	3	4	5
Strongly Disagree	Disagree	Neutral	Agree	Strongly Agree

28. I strive to create an environment where team members feel supported and empowered to succeed.

1	2	3	4	5
Strongly Disagree	Disagree	Neutral	Agree	Strongly Agree

29. I believe in the importance of actively listening to team members' concerns and ideas.

1	2	3	4	5
Strongly Disagree	Disagree	Neutral	Agree	Strongly Agree

30. I encourage team members to take ownership of their professional development and growth.

1	2	3	4	5
Strongly Disagree	Disagree	Neutral	Agree	Strongly Agree

31. I believe in the value of seeking out and considering diverse perspectives when making decisions.

1	2	3	4	5
Strongly Disagree	Disagree	Neutral	Agree	Strongly Agree

32. I strive to create an environment where team members feel comfortable taking smart risks.

1	2	3	4	5
Strongly Disagree	Disagree	Neutral	Agree	Strongly Agree

33. I believe in the importance of providing team members with the resources and support they need to succeed.

1	2	3	4	5
Strongly Disagree	Disagree	Neutral	Agree	Strongly Agree

34. I encourage team members to collaborate and share knowledge across the organization.

1	2	3	4	5
Strongly Disagree	Disagree	Neutral	Agree	Strongly Agree

35. I believe in the value of celebrating team members' individual strengths and contributions.

1	2	3	4	5
Strongly Disagree	Disagree	Neutral	Agree	Strongly Agree

36. I strive to create an environment where team members feel a sense of belonging and inclusion.

1	2	3	4	5
Strongly Disagree	Disagree	Neutral	Agree	Strongly Agree

37. I believe in the importance of leading by example and modeling the behaviors I expect from my team.

1	2	3	4	5
Strongly Disagree	Disagree	Neutral	Agree	Strongly Agree

38. I encourage team members to challenge the status quo and propose innovative solutions.

1	2	3	4	5
Strongly Disagree	Disagree	Neutral	Agree	Strongly Agree

39. I believe in the value of creating a culture of continuous learning and improvement within the team.

1	2	3	4	5
Strongly Disagree	Disagree	Neutral	Agree	Strongly Agree

40. I strive to create an environment where team members feel empowered to make a positive impact.

1	2	3	4	5
Strongly Disagree	Disagree	Neutral	Agree	Strongly Agree

Democratic Leadership

Totals

Strongly Disagree   1_____

Disagree   2_____

Neutral   3_____

Agree   4_____

Strongly Agree   5_____

Total

Democratic Personality Assessment _____

12.5 Authoritarian Leadership

1. I believe that as a leader, I should have the final say in all decisions.

1	2	3	4	5
Strongly Disagree	Disagree	Neutral	Agree	Strongly Agree

2. I expect my team members to follow my orders without question.

1	2	3	4	5
Strongly Disagree	Disagree	Neutral	Agree	Strongly Agree

3. I believe that strict discipline is necessary to maintain order and productivity.

1	2	3	4	5
Strongly Disagree	Disagree	Neutral	Agree	Strongly Agree

4. I think that team members should not challenge my authority or decisions.

1	2	3	4	5
Strongly Disagree	Disagree	Neutral	Agree	Strongly Agree

5. I believe that maintaining control over my team is more important than fostering collaboration.

1	2	3	4	5
Strongly Disagree	Disagree	Neutral	Agree	Strongly Agree

6. I expect my team members to prioritize work over their personal lives.

1	2	3	4	5
Strongly Disagree	Disagree	Neutral	Agree	Strongly Agree

7. I believe that punishment is an effective way to correct mistakes and maintain order.

1	2	3	4	5
Strongly Disagree	Disagree	Neutral	Agree	Strongly Agree

8. I think that showing vulnerability or admitting mistakes is a sign of weakness in a leader.

1	2	3	4	5
Strongly Disagree	Disagree	Neutral	Agree	Strongly Agree

9. I believe that my team members should conform to my way of doing things.

1	2	3	4	5
Strongly Disagree	Disagree	Neutral	Agree	Strongly Agree

10. I think that questioning my decisions is a sign of disloyalty or insubordination.

1	2	3	4	5
Strongly Disagree	Disagree	Neutral	Agree	Strongly Agree

11. I believe that I should closely monitor my team members' work to ensure they meet my standards.

1	2	3	4	5
Strongly Disagree	Disagree	Neutral	Agree	Strongly Agree

12. I think that my team members should sacrifice their personal goals for the goals of the organization.

1	2	3	4	5
Strongly Disagree	Disagree	Neutral	Agree	Strongly Agree

13. I believe that I should make all the important decisions without input from my team.

1	2	3	4	5
Strongly Disagree	Disagree	Neutral	Agree	Strongly Agree

14. I expect my team members to work long hours, even if it means sacrificing their work-life balance.

1	2	3	4	5
Strongly Disagree	Disagree	Neutral	Agree	Strongly Agree

15. I believe that I should be the one to set the goals and expectations for my team.

1	2	3	4	5
Strongly Disagree	Disagree	Neutral	Agree	Strongly Agree

16. I think that my team members should not question my authority, even if they disagree with me.

1	2	3	4	5
Strongly Disagree	Disagree	Neutral	Agree	Strongly Agree

17. I believe that I should have complete control over the flow of information within my team.

1	2	3	4	5
Strongly Disagree	Disagree	Neutral	Agree	Strongly Agree

18. I expect my team members to follow established rules and procedures without deviation.

1	2	3	4	5
Strongly Disagree	Disagree	Neutral	Agree	Strongly Agree

19. I think that creativity and innovation should be discouraged if they go against my vision.

1	2	3	4	5
Strongly Disagree	Disagree	Neutral	Agree	Strongly Agree

20. I believe that I should be the one to assign tasks and roles to my team members.

1	2	3	4	5
Strongly Disagree	Disagree	Neutral	Agree	Strongly Agree

21. I expect my team members to report all issues and concerns directly to me.

1	2	3	4	5
Strongly Disagree	Disagree	Neutral	Agree	Strongly Agree

22. I think that my team members should not engage in activities or relationships that I haven't approved.

1	2	3	4	5
Strongly Disagree	Disagree	Neutral	Agree	Strongly Agree

23. I believe that I should be the one to evaluate my team members' performance.

1	2	3	4	5
Strongly Disagree	Disagree	Neutral	Agree	Strongly Agree

24. I expect my team members to follow my leadership without question, even if they have doubts.

1	2	3	4	5
Strongly Disagree	Disagree	Neutral	Agree	Strongly Agree

25. I think that my team members should prioritize the organization's needs over their own.

1	2	3	4	5
Strongly Disagree	Disagree	Neutral	Agree	Strongly Agree

26. I believe that I should have the power to hire, fire, and promote team members as I see fit.

1	2	3	4	5
Strongly Disagree	Disagree	Neutral	Agree	Strongly Agree

27. I expect my team members to conform to the organization's culture and values without question.

1	2	3	4	5
Strongly Disagree	Disagree	Neutral	Agree	Strongly Agree

28. I think that my team members should not challenge the status quo or established processes.

1	2	3	4	5
Strongly Disagree	Disagree	Neutral	Agree	Strongly Agree

29. I believe that I should be the one to determine the priorities and goals for my team.

1	2	3	4	5
Strongly Disagree	Disagree	Neutral	Agree	Strongly Agree

30. I expect my team members to put the organization's interests above their own personal interests.

1	2	3	4	5
Strongly Disagree	Disagree	Neutral	Agree	Strongly Agree

31. I think that my team members should not question my decisions, even if they have relevant information or expertise.

1	2	3	4	5
Strongly Disagree	Disagree	Neutral	Agree	Strongly Agree

32. I believe that I should have complete control over the resources allocated to my team.

1	2	3	4	5
Strongly Disagree	Disagree	Neutral	Agree	Strongly Agree

33. I expect my team members to follow my instructions precisely, without deviation or improvisation.

1	2	3	4	5
Strongly Disagree	Disagree	Neutral	Agree	Strongly Agree

34. I think that my team members should not share information or collaborate with other teams without my approval.

1	2	3	4	5
Strongly Disagree	Disagree	Neutral	Agree	Strongly Agree

35. I believe that I should be the one to determine the methods and approaches used by my team.

1	2	3	4	5
Strongly Disagree	Disagree	Neutral	Agree	Strongly Agree

36. I expect my team members to prioritize the completion of tasks over their own wellbeing or satisfaction.

1	2	3	4	5
Strongly Disagree	Disagree	Neutral	Agree	Strongly Agree

37. I think that my team members should not seek feedback or input from others without my permission.

1	2	3	4	5
Strongly Disagree	Disagree	Neutral	Agree	Strongly Agree

38. I believe that I should be the one to determine the standards of quality and performance for my team.

1	2	3	4	5
Strongly Disagree	Disagree	Neutral	Agree	Strongly Agree

39. I expect my team members to follow established hierarchies and chains of command without question.

1	2	3	4	5
Strongly Disagree	Disagree	Neutral	Agree	Strongly Agree

40. I think that my team members should prioritize obedience and loyalty to me above all else.

1	2	3	4	5
Strongly Disagree	Disagree	Neutral	Agree	Strongly Agree

Authoritarian Leadership

Totals

Strongly Disagree   1_____

Disagree   2_____

Neutral   3_____

Agree   4_____

Strongly Agree   5_____

Total

Authoritarian Personality Assessment _____

12.6 Laissez-Faire Leadership

1. I believe in giving team members complete freedom to make decisions.

1	2	3	4	5
Strongly Disagree	Disagree	Neutral	Agree	Strongly Agree

2. I rarely intervene in the day-to-day activities of my team.

1	2	3	4	5
Strongly Disagree	Disagree	Neutral	Agree	Strongly Agree

3. I trust my team members to solve problems on their own.

1	2	3	4	5
Strongly Disagree	Disagree	Neutral	Agree	Strongly Agree

4. I believe that team members should take full responsibility for their work.

1	2	3	4	5
Strongly Disagree	Disagree	Neutral	Agree	Strongly Agree

5. I avoid providing direct guidance or instructions to my team.

1	2	3	4	5
Strongly Disagree	Disagree	Neutral	Agree	Strongly Agree

6. I believe that team members should be self-motivated and self-directed.

1	2	3	4	5
Strongly Disagree	Disagree	Neutral	Agree	Strongly Agree

7. I rarely enforce deadlines or strict performance standards.

1	2	3	4	5
Strongly Disagree	Disagree	Neutral	Agree	Strongly Agree

8. I believe that team members should have the autonomy to set their own goals.

1	2	3	4	5
Strongly Disagree	Disagree	Neutral	Agree	Strongly Agree

9. I avoid making decisions unless absolutely necessary.

1	2	3	4	5
Strongly Disagree	Disagree	Neutral	Agree	Strongly Agree

10. I believe that team members should be trusted to manage their own workload.

1	2	3	4	5
Strongly Disagree	Disagree	Neutral	Agree	Strongly Agree

11. I rarely provide feedback or performance evaluations to my team.

1	2	3	4	5
Strongly Disagree	Disagree	Neutral	Agree	Strongly Agree

12. I believe that team members should be free to determine their own work methods.

1	2	3	4	5
Strongly Disagree	Disagree	Neutral	Agree	Strongly Agree

13. I avoid setting clear expectations or guidelines for my team.

1	2	3	4	5
Strongly Disagree	Disagree	Neutral	Agree	Strongly Agree

14. I believe that team members should be allowed to work at their own pace.

1	2	3	4	5
Strongly Disagree	Disagree	Neutral	Agree	Strongly Agree

15. I rarely monitor the progress or performance of my team.

1	2	3	4	5
Strongly Disagree	Disagree	Neutral	Agree	Strongly Agree

16. I believe that team members should be trusted to resolve conflicts on their own.

1	2	3	4	5
Strongly Disagree	Disagree	Neutral	Agree	Strongly Agree

17. I avoid providing praise or recognition for individual or team achievements.

1	2	3	4	5
Strongly Disagree	Disagree	Neutral	Agree	Strongly Agree

18. I believe that team members should be free to take risks without fear of consequences.

1	2	3	4	5
Strongly Disagree	Disagree	Neutral	Agree	Strongly Agree

19. I rarely communicate my vision or long-term goals to my team.

1	2	3	4	5
Strongly Disagree	Disagree	Neutral	Agree	Strongly Agree

20. I believe that team members should be trusted to prioritize their own tasks.

1	2	3	4	5
Strongly Disagree	Disagree	Neutral	Agree	Strongly Agree

21. I avoid providing support or resources unless specifically requested.

1	2	3	4	5
Strongly Disagree	Disagree	Neutral	Agree	Strongly Agree

22. I believe that team members should be free to determine their own work schedules.

1	2	3	4	5
Strongly Disagree	Disagree	Neutral	Agree	Strongly Agree

23. I rarely engage in team-building or collaborative activities.

1	2	3	4	5
Strongly Disagree	Disagree	Neutral	Agree	Strongly Agree

24. I believe that team members should be trusted to manage their own professional development.

1	2	3	4	5
Strongly Disagree	Disagree	Neutral	Agree	Strongly Agree

25. I avoid setting performance metrics or targets for my team.

1	2	3	4	5
Strongly Disagree	Disagree	Neutral	Agree	Strongly Agree

26. I believe that team members should be free to determine their own roles and responsibilities.

1	2	3	4	5
Strongly Disagree	Disagree	Neutral	Agree	Strongly Agree

27. I rarely provide guidance or mentorship to individual team members.

1	2	3	4	5
Strongly Disagree	Disagree	Neutral	Agree	Strongly Agree

28. I believe that team members should be trusted to manage their own stress and well-being.

1	2	3	4	5
Strongly Disagree	Disagree	Neutral	Agree	Strongly Agree

29. I avoid intervening in team dynamics or interpersonal conflicts.

1	2	3	4	5
Strongly Disagree	Disagree	Neutral	Agree	Strongly Agree

30. I believe that team members should be free to determine their own work-life balance.

1	2	3	4	5
Strongly Disagree	Disagree	Neutral	Agree	Strongly Agree

31. I rarely provide updates or communicate changes to my team.

1	2	3	4	5
Strongly Disagree	Disagree	Neutral	Agree	Strongly Agree

32. I believe that team members should be trusted to manage their own resources and budgets.

1	2	3	4	5
Strongly Disagree	Disagree	Neutral	Agree	Strongly Agree

33. I avoid setting agendas or leading team meetings.

1	2	3	4	5
Strongly Disagree	Disagree	Neutral	Agree	Strongly Agree

34. I believe that team members should be free to determine their own training and development needs.

1	2	3	4	5
Strongly Disagree	Disagree	Neutral	Agree	Strongly Agree

35. I rarely provide input or direction on project planning or execution.

1	2	3	4	5
Strongly Disagree	Disagree	Neutral	Agree	Strongly Agree

36. I believe that team members should be trusted to manage their own stakeholder relationships.

1	2	3	4	5
Strongly Disagree	Disagree	Neutral	Agree	Strongly Agree

37. I avoid setting or enforcing team norms or behavioral expectations.

1	2	3	4	5
Strongly Disagree	Disagree	Neutral	Agree	Strongly Agree

38. I believe that team members should be free to determine their own career paths and advancement.

1	2	3	4	5
Strongly Disagree	Disagree	Neutral	Agree	Strongly Agree

39. I rarely celebrate or acknowledge team successes or milestones.

1	2	3	4	5
Strongly Disagree	Disagree	Neutral	Agree	Strongly Agree

40. I believe that team members should be trusted to manage their own performance and accountability.

1	2	3	4	5
Strongly Disagree	Disagree	Neutral	Agree	Strongly Agree

Laissez-Faire Leadership

Totals

Strongly Disagree	1_____
Disagree	2_____
Neutral	3_____
Agree	4_____
Strongly Agree	5_____

Total

Laissez-Faire Personality Assessment _____

12.7 Charismatic Leadership

1. I inspire others with my vision and enthusiasm.

1	2	3	4	5
Strongly Disagree	Disagree	Neutral	Agree	Strongly Agree

2. I have a strong sense of purpose and mission that I communicate effectively to my team.

1	2	3	4	5
Strongly Disagree	Disagree	Neutral	Agree	Strongly Agree

3. I lead by example and demonstrate the behaviors I expect from my team.

1	2	3	4	5
Strongly Disagree	Disagree	Neutral	Agree	Strongly Agree

4. I have a compelling presence that captures people's attention and inspires them to follow me.

1	2	3	4	5
Strongly Disagree	Disagree	Neutral	Agree	Strongly Agree

5. I communicate with passion and conviction, which motivates others to take action.

1	2	3	4	5
Strongly Disagree	Disagree	Neutral	Agree	Strongly Agree

6. I have a clear set of values and beliefs that guide my leadership and decision-making.

1	2	3	4	5
Strongly Disagree	Disagree	Neutral	Agree	Strongly Agree

7. I create a sense of shared identity and purpose within my team.

1	2	3	4	5
Strongly Disagree	Disagree	Neutral	Agree	Strongly Agree

8. I inspire trust and loyalty among my team members through my actions and words.

1	2	3	4	5
Strongly Disagree	Disagree	Neutral	Agree	Strongly Agree

9. I have a strong emotional connection with my team members, which enhances their commitment to our goals.

1	2	3	4	5
Strongly Disagree	Disagree	Neutral	Agree	Strongly Agree

10. I communicate a compelling vision of the future that inspires others to work towards it.

1	2	3	4	5
Strongly Disagree	Disagree	Neutral	Agree	Strongly Agree

11. I demonstrate confidence and optimism, even in the face of challenges or setbacks.

1	2	3	4	5
Strongly Disagree	Disagree	Neutral	Agree	Strongly Agree

12. I have a charismatic personality that naturally draws people to me and my ideas.

1	2	3	4	5
Strongly Disagree	Disagree	Neutral	Agree	Strongly Agree

13. I create a sense of urgency and momentum that drives my team to achieve exceptional results.

1	2	3	4	5
Strongly Disagree	Disagree	Neutral	Agree	Strongly Agree

14. I appeal to my team members' emotions and values to inspire their best work.

1	2	3	4	5
Strongly Disagree	Disagree	Neutral	Agree	Strongly Agree

15. I have a strong sense of charisma that enables me to influence and persuade others.

1	2	3	4	5
Strongly Disagree	Disagree	Neutral	Agree	Strongly Agree

16. I create a culture of excellence and continuous improvement within my team.

1	2	3	4	5
Strongly Disagree	Disagree	Neutral	Agree	Strongly Agree

17. I inspire my team members to think creatively and innovatively to solve problems.

1	2	3	4	5
Strongly Disagree	Disagree	Neutral	Agree	Strongly Agree

18. I have a strong presence that commands attention and respect from others.

1	2	3	4	5
Strongly Disagree	Disagree	Neutral	Agree	Strongly Agree

19. I create a sense of meaning and purpose in my team members' work.

1	2	3	4	5
Strongly Disagree	Disagree	Neutral	Agree	Strongly Agree

20. I inspire my team members to take ownership and responsibility for their work.

1	2	3	4	5
Strongly Disagree	Disagree	Neutral	Agree	Strongly Agree

21. I have a magnetic personality that attracts talented individuals to my team.

1	2	3	4	5
Strongly Disagree	Disagree	Neutral	Agree	Strongly Agree

22. I create a sense of excitement and energy within my team that drives performance.

1	2	3	4	5
Strongly Disagree	Disagree	Neutral	Agree	Strongly Agree

23. I inspire my team members to stretch beyond their comfort zones and achieve their full potential.

1	2	3	4	5
Strongly Disagree	Disagree	Neutral	Agree	Strongly Agree

24. I have a strong vision that I articulate in a way that resonates with my team members.

1	2	3	4	5
Strongly Disagree	Disagree	Neutral	Agree	Strongly Agree

25. I create a culture of trust and psychological safety within my team.

1	2	3	4	5
Strongly Disagree	Disagree	Neutral	Agree	Strongly Agree

26. I inspire my team members to be passionate and committed to our shared goals.

1	2	3	4	5
Strongly Disagree	Disagree	Neutral	Agree	Strongly Agree

27. I have a strong personal brand that enhances my credibility and influence as a leader.

1	2	3	4	5
Strongly Disagree	Disagree	Neutral	Agree	Strongly Agree

28. I create a sense of loyalty and dedication among my team members.

1	2	3	4	5
Strongly Disagree	Disagree	Neutral	Agree	Strongly Agree

29. I inspire my team members to be resilient and persevere in the face of challenges.

1	2	3	4	5
Strongly Disagree	Disagree	Neutral	Agree	Strongly Agree

30. I have a strong stage presence that enables me to deliver compelling presentations and speeches.

1	2	3	4	5
Strongly Disagree	Disagree	Neutral	Agree	Strongly Agree

31. I create a sense of community and belonging within my team.

1	2	3	4	5
Strongly Disagree	Disagree	Neutral	Agree	Strongly Agree

32. I inspire my team members to be proactive and take initiative in their work.

1	2	3	4	5
Strongly Disagree	Disagree	Neutral	Agree	Strongly Agree

33. I have a strong ability to read and respond to my team members' emotions and needs.

1	2	3	4	5
Strongly Disagree	Disagree	Neutral	Agree	Strongly Agree

34. I create a sense of pride and fulfillment among my team members in their work.

1	2	3	4	5
Strongly Disagree	Disagree	Neutral	Agree	Strongly Agree

35. I inspire my team members to be adaptable and embrace change.

1	2	3	4	5
Strongly Disagree	Disagree	Neutral	Agree	Strongly Agree

36. I have a strong ability to build and leverage relationships to achieve my goals.

1	2	3	4	5
Strongly Disagree	Disagree	Neutral	Agree	Strongly Agree

37. I create a sense of purpose and meaning that extends beyond individual roles and responsibilities.

1	2	3	4	5
Strongly Disagree	Disagree	Neutral	Agree	Strongly Agree

38. I inspire my team members to be collaborative and work effectively with others.

1	2	3	4	5
Strongly Disagree	Disagree	Neutral	Agree	Strongly Agree

39. I have a strong ability to inspire and motivate others, even in challenging circumstances.

1	2	3	4	5
Strongly Disagree	Disagree	Neutral	Agree	Strongly Agree

40. I create a sense of purpose and meaning that inspires my team members to give their best effort.

1	2	3	4	5
Strongly Disagree	Disagree	Neutral	Agree	Strongly Agree

Charismatic Leadership

Totals

Strongly Disagree	1 _____
Disagree	2 _____
Neutral	3 _____
Agree	4 _____
Strongly Agree	5 _____

Total

Charismatic Personality Assessment _____

DCS5 Personality Assessment Results

Servant _____

Democratic _____

Authoritarian _____

Laissez-Faire _____

Charismatic _____

It is important to note that individuals may exhibit characteristics of multiple leadership styles, and scores should be interpreted as tendencies rather than absolute classifications. A higher total score indicates a stronger alignment with that specific leadership style.

The insights gained from these surveys can help leaders and stakeholders recognize their strengths, identify potential blind spots, and develop a more well-rounded and effective leadership approach based on their unique context and goals.

Conclusion

Whether leading in-person or virtually, in times of stability or change, in pursuit of efficiency or innovation, quality leaders inspire and empower their teams to achieve their full potential, and to contribute to something greater than themselves. They do so by setting a clear and compelling vision, building strong and trusting relationships, making data-driven and customer-centric decisions, and fostering a culture of continuous learning and improvement. Most importantly, they lead with integrity, compassion, and a deep commitment to serving others and making a positive impact on the world.

There is an undeniable importance of ethical leadership. The fabric of trust and integrity within an organization largely depends on leaders who prioritize ethical standards and transparent practices. This book has underscored the value of holding effective meetings, fostering ethical behavior, and fully leveraging the diverse traits of employees. These elements are not just foundational; they are transformative, influencing every level of organizational culture and performance.

Implement the leadership styles and strategies that resonate most with your personal and organizational goals. Cultivate a culture of continuous learning and adaptation. The landscape of leadership is ever-evolving, and staying abreast of these changes is crucial for your growth and the success of your team.

Lead with integrity and purpose. Embrace the challenges that come with leadership roles, using them as stepping stones to build resilience and adaptability. Your commitment to ethical principles and your ability to adapt to the needs of your people will set the tone for your legacy - aim to leave a lasting positive impact on your teams and your entire organization.

Your greatest return on investment is the people you lead. How you guide, support, and inspire them will chart the course of your collective success. Embark on your leadership journey with confidence, equipped with the knowledge that you have the tools and insights to lead effectively. Transform potential into excellence, one leadership decision at a time.

Some key themes that emerge across these leadership styles include the importance of adaptability, collaboration, innovation, and customer focus. Leaders who are able to pivot quickly in response to changing circumstances, engage their teams in problem-solving and decision-making, foster a culture of creativity and experimentation, and prioritize the needs and feedback of customers are more likely to drive long-term success and sustainability for their organizations.

These styles also highlight some of the common challenges and risks associated with different leadership styles, such as resistance to change, communication breakdowns, overemphasis on short-term results, and neglect of employee well-being and development. Leaders must be mindful of these potential pitfalls and take proactive steps to mitigate them, such as setting clear expectations, providing adequate resources and support, modeling desired behaviors, and seeking feedback and input from their teams.

No single leadership style is a panacea for all situations. Rather, the most effective leaders are those who are able to adapt their approach based on the specific needs, goals, and constraints of their context. This requires a deep understanding of one's own strengths and limitations as a leader, as well as a willingness to learn from others and experiment with different techniques and tools.

Emphasize the importance of balancing different priorities and stakeholder interests when leading organizations. Leaders must often navigate the tensions between short-term efficiency and long-term innovation, between process consistency and individual creativity, between customer satisfaction and employee well-being, and between organizational growth and social responsibility. Finding the right balance requires ongoing reflection, dialogue, and adjustment, as well as a clear sense of purpose and values.

Finally, these wide variety of styles underscore the critical role that leadership plays in shaping the culture, performance, and impact of organizations. Leaders set the tone, direction, and expectations for their teams, and have a disproportionate influence on the attitudes, behaviors, and outcomes of their employees. As such, leadership is not just a position or a set of skills, but a profound responsibility and opportunity to make a positive difference in the lives of others and the world at large.

In today's complex, dynamic, and interconnected business environment, the need for effective, ethical, and adaptable leadership has never been greater. By studying and applying the insights and lessons from these different leadership styles, and by continually developing their own self-awareness, empathy, and agility, leaders can rise to the challenges and opportunities of the 21st century, and create lasting value for their organizations and stakeholders.

In the end, leadership is not about titles, power, or prestige, but about the ability to influence, motivate, and enable others to achieve shared goals and create meaningful change. It is a journey of self-discovery, growth, and service, that requires ongoing reflection, feedback, and adaptation. By embracing this journey with curiosity, courage, and humility, and by leveraging the insights and lessons from these different leadership styles, leaders can unlock their own potential and that of their teams, and make a lasting difference in their organizations and communities.

Diane Schildgen

References

Management vs. Leadership: What's the Difference?

https://www.ollusa.edu/blog/management-vs-leadership.html#:~:text=Focus%3A%20Leadership%20zeros%20in%20on,concentrates%20on%20short%2Dterm%20objectives.

The Impact of Digitization and Technology on Leadership
https://globalcoachgroup.com/the-impact-of-digitization-and-technology-on-leadership/

4 Examples of Ethical Leadership in Business - HBS Online
https://online.hbs.edu/blog/post/examples-of-ethical-leadership

Use motivation theory to inspire your team's best work
https://www.atlassian.com/blog/leadership/motivation-theory

7 servant leadership examples in business to inspire and ...
https://www.skillpacks.com/servant-leadership-examples-in-business/

How to Make Different Business Leadership Styles Work (With Case Studies) https://mariopeshev.com/business-leadership-styles-case-studies/

When Is Authoritarian Leadership Less Detrimental? The ...
https://www.ncbi.nlm.nih.gov/pmc/articles/PMC9819526/

Authoritarian vs Laissez-Faire Leadership: Pros and Cons
https://m.economictimes.com/jobs/c-suite/authoritarian-vs-laissez-faire-leadership-prosand-cons/articleshow/104732593.cms

Research: How Cultural Differences Can Impact Global Teams

https://hbr.org/2021/06/research-how-cultural-differences-can-impact-global-teams

Beyond Generational Differences: The New Workforce
https://executiveeducation.wharton.upenn.edu/thought-leadership/wharton-atwork/2023/12/beyond-generational-differences/

What Great Remote Managers Do Differently
https://hbr.org/2022/10/what-great-remotemanagers-do-differently

Crisis Leadership: Strategies for Navigating Turbulent Times
https://m.economictimes.com/jobs/c-suite/crisis-leadership-strategies-for-navigatingturbulent-times/articleshow/104625755.cms

How to set effective team goals (with examples) - Mural
https://www.mural.co/blog/team-goals

Strength-Based Leadership: 34 Traits Of Successful Leaders
https://positivepsychology.com/strength-based-leadership/

How to Delegate Effectively: 9 Tips for Managers - HBS Online
https://online.hbs.edu/blog/post/how-to-delegate-effectively

Preventing and Managing Team Conflict
https://professional.dce.harvard.edu/blog/preventing-and-managing-team-conflict/

9 effective self-assessment tools for leadership roles
https://uk.indeed.com/careeradvice/career-development/self-assessment-tools-for-leadership

The Power Of Vulnerability In Leadership: Experts Say ...

https://www.forbes.com/sites/luisromero/2023/03/08/the-power-of-vulnerability-inleadership-experts-say-authenticity-and-honesty-can-move-people-and-achieve-results/ How CEOs Manage Time https://hbr.org/2018/07/how-ceos-manage-time

Emotional Intelligence Training for Leaders - Ccl.org
https://www.ccl.org/leadershipsolutions/leadership-topics/emotional-intelligence-training/

Types & Importance of Risk Taking in Entrepreneurship 2024
https://www.nexford.edu/insights/risk-taking-in-entrepreneurship

7 reasons why a vision statement is important - LinkedIn
https://www.linkedin.com/pulse/7-reasons-why-vision-statement-important-pandekgroup-

limited#:~:text=A%20vision%20statement%20marks%20the,%2C%20and%20non%2Dp rofit%20needs.

How to Instill a Coaching Culture - Ccl.org
https://www.ccl.org/articles/leadingeffectively-articles/instill-coaching-culture/

How Diversity Can Drive Innovation
https://hbr.org/2013/12/how-diversity-can-driveinnovation

Using the Ethical Leadership Decision-Making Framework
https://www.airuniversity.af.edu/Wild-Blue-Yonder/Articles/Article

The Case For Transparency In The Workplace, And Its ...

https://www.forbes.com/sites/forbesbusinesscouncil/2023/06/16/the-case-fortransparency-in-the-workplace-and-its-impact-on-organizational-performance/

Why Integrity is so Important in Leadership.
https://www.linkedin.com/pulse/whyintegrity-so-important-leadership-lorenzo-flores

4 Examples of Ethical Leadership in Business - HBS Online
https://online.hbs.edu/blog/post/examples-of-ethical-leadership

Use Active Listening Skills to Coach Others
https://www.ccl.org/articles/leadingeffectively-articles/coaching-others-use-active-listening-skills/

How to adapt communication for cultural differences

https://theewgroup.com/us/blog/adapt-communication-cultural-differences/

The Importance Of Empathy In Leadership: How To Lead ...
https://www.forbes.com/sites/karadennison/2023/02/24/the-importance-of-empathy-inleadership-how-to-lead-with-compassion-and-understanding-in-2023/

How to Communicate Professionally and Digitally - LinkedIn
https://www.linkedin.com/advice/0/what-best-practices-professional-digital

A Leader's Framework for Decision Making
https://hbr.org/2007/11/a-leadersframework-for-decision-making

10 principles of leading change management
https://www.strategybusiness.com/article/00255

Must-Know Leadership KPIs - Gitnux
https://gitnux.org/leadership-

kpis/#:~:text=Common%20Leadership%20KPIs%20include%20employee,turnover%20r ate%20attributable%20to%20leadership.

How to Spot — and Develop — High-Potential Talent in Your Organization https://hbr.org/2022/05/how-to-spot-and-develop-high-potential-talent-in-yourorganization

The 7 Elements of an Impactful Leadership Development ...
https://voxy.com/blog/leadership-development-program/

Leadership Styles and Their Impact on Organizational Culture
https://m.economictimes.com/jobs/c-suite/leadership-styles-and-their-impact-onorganizational-culture/articleshow/104632282.cms

Leaving Your Mark: Leadership Legacy Examples
https://www.catalystecr.com/blog/leadership-legacy-examples/

www.ingramcontent.com/pod-product-compliance
Lightning Source LLC
Chambersburg PA
CBHW050200230526
45470CB00001B/179